HOURS OF PURE GOLD

My Weekend with the Masters of Motivation
A Story of Inspiration, Motivation, and Gratitude

KANDI A. WHITE

Copyright © 2023 by Kandi A. White. All rights reserved.

All rights reserved. No part of this book may be reproduced or transmitted in any form or by any means, electronic or mechanical, including photocopying, recording, or by any information storage and retrieval system without express written permission from the author, except in the case of brief quotations embodied in critical reviews and certain other noncommercial uses permitted by copyright law.

Published in the United States of America

Brilliant Books Literary
137 Forest Park Lane Thomasville
North Carolina 27360 USA

ISBN:
Paperback: 979-8-88945-234-8
E-Book: 979-8-88945-235-5

Contents

Dedication 5
Foreword 9
Introduction 13
Tribute 25

1   Journey to Santa Clara 27
2   BLASST Is a Reality 32
3   An "Aha" Experience with Dr. Wayne W. Dyer 37
4   I'm Going to Firewalk 48
5   Why Am I Here—It's More Than Lunch! 53
6   Master Coaching with Gary Shawkey and Dr. Sylvia Williams 57
7   The Fullness of Truth with Dr. Wayne W. Dyer 61
8   Fulfill Your Dreams with Les Brown and . . . Never Give Up with Denice Young 66
9   Do the Right Thing with David Lawrence 74
10   Change Your Economic Future with Jim Rohn 78

11	How to Cultivate an Endless Referral of Customers with Bob Burg	85
12	Taking Risks with David Miln Smith	90
13	Fundamentals of Success with Jim Rohn	96
14	The Key to Success with John Amatt	103
15	Event Finale . . . Can It Get Better Than This?	109
16	The Story Is Told . . . The Journey Continues	112
Author Bio		121

Dedication

"Praise God from whom all blessings flow."
Doxology

Thank you, Lord.

This book is dedicated to a group of people who, over a four-day period, February 6–10, 2003, made a profound impact on my life. To say I had a life-changing experience in the presence of these people is an understatement.

I attended an event called BLASST, Building Leadership and Super Success Training, in Santa Clara, California, the brainchild of Mr. Gary Shawkey. The motivational speakers that attended empowered us by their experiences to take our personal and professional lives, aspirations, and dreams to the next level. My expectations were far surpassed, and I would like to share the information I learned with you. I consider it a blessing and a privilege.

Their inspiring stories are more than just results. Each has a unique story to tell about their challenges and successes. Something that stands out is their belief in achieving their goals, their focus, their enjoyment and passion to help others achieve their goals and dreams. This really falls in line with the desires of my heart.

Some aspects of their teachings that have been reinforced in my personal and professional life are the need to plan, market, and improve.

Plan	-	Plan your goals, write them down, and have the right attitude.
Market the plan	-	Begin putting the plan in action. Take the first step however small it may be. Find suitable resources. Talk to successful people and learn from them. Test different methods. Read, read, and read some more.
Improve	-	Measure success through evaluation of the results. Start again or replan with a new process if the first one failed and the belief is still strong. Speak with your team, get advice, and plan again. Don't give *up*! And in all things pray and give thanks to God.

These men and women are all masters in their field, and for each of them I have much respect, and gratitude.

Dr. Wayne W. Dyer
Dr. Sylvia Williams
David Lawrence
Les Brown
Denice Young
Jim Rohn
David Miln Smith
Bob Burg
John Amatt

Hours of Pure Gold

There stood an angel too whose voice sang to my heart.

Skye Dyer

    And certainly I have to thank all the wonderful people I met who are now everlasting friends.
    May God continue to strengthen and bless you in all of your endeavors.

Foreword

Affiliate marketing, network marketing, multilevel marketing, Internet marketing, social media marketing. These are common buzz words that you would find on the Internet today. Put these words in any search engine and you would get access to thousands of websites. One of the reasons I wrote this book is my passion for being involved in some of these programs, which I will introduce to you. I say passion because I really enjoy marketing on the Internet for the relationships I've developed, being able to help others, and the freedom to explore and use my God given talents and skills. It's a personal business as well. When you have a passion for something, it doesn't seem like work at all. I'm enthusiastic about my passions and can speak about them for hours.

I also have another passion and reason for writing this book. That reason is to give thanks to God, my creator, for his love, for not giving up on me and for all the wonderful opportunities and blessings this experience has given me. Because I am so thankful, I want to give something back to my community and, indeed, the world. I've always said: "If I pass through this life on earth and know that I have helped someone in some way, then I know my life has a purpose."

I live in Bermuda, a very small island out in the Atlantic Ocean. We have people of many cultures living on the island. I am blessed to have been born here. I love to worship at a small Anglican Church called St. Monica's. The island is divided into nine parishes across twenty-one square miles of land joined by several bridges. St. Monica's is one of the Anglican churches in the Parish of Pembroke.

Some prayers I have for *Hours of Pure Gold* are:

1. That as I share this information with you, you will find these real-life experiences helpful, motivating, and inspiring. That with the help of the teachings of these speakers you can build self-esteem, become motivated, formulate clear goals, and enjoy the things you long to do. If you're looking for more success in your business, family, social or personal life, these leaders have proven techniques and action steps for you. Listening to their wit and wisdom has opened up a field of opportunities for me to grasp and nurture, and I believe it can do the same for you.
2. That as you read, you will be encouraged to start or finish the projects you've been putting off; that you will make positive changes in your life; that you will believe you can achieve whatever you put your mind to, and you will know there are resources and people along the way who can and are willing to help you.
3. That through this experience and purchasing this book you will know you've helped with our vision and will want to share it with others. You may want to help us in other ways, by praying for us, sending us an encouraging email, worshipping with us from near or far. God has promised us

abundance and to fulfill the desires of our hearts. All we have to do is ask him and to be faithful unto him. As I get to know God more and more each day, he fills my heart with love and peace, and nothing is more fulfilling to me. All other blessings I consider a bonus and I give thanks.
4. That the love of God may fill your hearts and minds, and he will reveal your true purpose for your life.

As Gary Shawkey reminded us,

"Live to be Outstanding!"

Introduction

Let me set the stage and give you some information on my passion for Internet marketing and how I arrived at this beautiful city called San Francisco, traveling to and staying in Santa Clara in the heart of Silicon Valley.

I will mention some people who have touched my life in a special way and have helped me become the person I am today.

I grew up in Bermuda like any normal child. My loving mom worked hard day and night to provide for her children—four girls—and for her extended family as well. There was always plenty of people visiting our small apartment, and there was always good food. Mom loves to cook and cooks as if she's feeding five thousand. Growing up, there were certain things we could not afford, as Mom's jobs were seasonal. But Mom loved to sew and knit, so you would always see my sisters and I decked out in a pretty outfit that she made for us with love. Of course we had the big ribbons in our hair—more ribbon than hair most of the time.

As far back as I can remember, I always had the desire, the drive, the determination that I would make my life better and someday help my mother. I would challenge myself to take the next step to get to the next level.

I excelled in anything I put my heart and mind into, be it sports, school, or work.

And as I look back, I could have made a few adjustments and done some things differently, but I have no regrets really. It was all part of growth.

At the early age of fourteen, I had a wonderful opportunity to attend the summer Olympics in Montreal, Canada, with a group called Young Life. I love sports, and I knew it would be a trip of a lifetime. I remember working hard getting sponsors for trashathons, bake sales, and car washes to raise money for the trip. After a week in Montreal, the group of us traveled by bus and cars to a Christian outreach camp called Windy Gap. Windy Gap is in the Smokey Mountains of North Carolina, USA. The camp is for teenagers and is run by Young Life. Whilst at the camp, I made the best decision in my life. That was to give my heart to God and follow him. Having been brought up in the Anglican Church in Bermuda, I had the seeds planted that were nurtured into a new relationship with Jesus.

I came home from camp, and I told my mom I was a Christian—one of the scariest things I had ever done. I didn't know if I would be laughed at or ridiculed. That trip was the beginning of my journey to start a new life. There have been hills and valleys along the way. There have been times when God should have expelled me, but instead he loved me for all that I am and will be.

There was a man, the late Francis Gosling—Goose as we called him—who started Young Life in Bermuda several years before I went on the trip to Windy Gap. I came to love and respect Goose. He was a devoted Christian, and although he never married or had children of his own, we were all considered his children. His house was open to all who would come to Young Life meetings and Bible studies. Goose, I love you, and I know you are surrounded by God's angels.

At eighteen, I met a young man who, eleven years later, became my soul mate. Morris, my love, best friend, and husband, is a person who taught me the importance of communicating my feelings. For that, I will always be grateful. You see, I'm really a private person, and I kept a lot of things inside. Morris and I were married by Canon Nisbett, which was a dream come true. We have two beautiful children, Amber and Tristan, whom we love and adore.

Around the time I got married, I was asked by the superintendent of our Sunday school if I would like to become a Sunday school teacher. This special lady, Newvilla Dill, has become a mentor to me. She did so much for the children at our Sunday school and continues to serve our church faithfully. She has a very special gift for singing and playing the piano. Newvilla always seems to challenge me. Whenever she asks me to do something, whether it be preparing the children's story for family service or printing a bookmark, I always say yes. Then I cling to Phil. 4:13, one of my favorite scriptures, "For I can do anything God asks me to with the help of Christ who gives me the strength and power." Only by God's help, power, and strength am I able to accomplish these things as well as write this book.

Also at eighteen, I started working full-time at the Bank of Bermuda. Throughout my career, I consistently raised the level of my performance to get to the next level to provide the desires of my heart and to prepare for my family's future.

Along with working full-time, I've always had an entrepreneurial spirit. I often dreamt of working for myself, not necessarily by myself but on my own terms. My mom Brenda, Morris, and I started a home-based printing business in 1986, but I basically ran it myself. A few years ago, I bought a new computer and ventured into the world of the Internet. Oh boy, money well spent! I can't remember exactly how I got there, but I came across a website called Streamline International. Streamline was a company who had everything I was looking for, a way to build a financial future. It had great health products and an excellent pay plan, or so I thought anyway. The write-up was very convincing, and I was very naïve. I'm glad to say I've matured a bit from experience.

Not knowing a thing about what I was doing, I joined Streamline as an affiliate marketer and spent some serious money in search of financial independence. There are thousands of websites on the Internet that are full of hype, and some are scams as well. You must be careful and do as much research as you can about the company before joining or spending your money. Stay away from websites that have no contact details like a telephone number and address. Call the number and ensure that it is answered, if you must leave a message, does the call get returned and on a timely basis. There are many ways in which a company could set up its affiliate business. Basically, a company or person has a great product or service to sell or promote. In order to reach the masses of people they get others (affiliates) to help them and in return pay a commission for making sales or bringing in new affiliates.

As an affiliate for Streamline, the commissions came from buying and selling their products. I could also get a percentage of the commissions of other affiliates I introduced to the company. I started getting $5 commission checks, and I got several more $5 commission checks. By the time bank charges were deducted, the check wasn't worth anything, so I stopped cashing them. Streamline eventually went bust, but I was enjoying this Internet stuff. I looked for another opportunity and perhaps another.

In June 2001, I joined a program called "Big Dogs." Big Dogs was intended to be the mother load of all lead-generating programs. If you needed unlimited leads to send information about your programs, you needed to sign up for the various lead-generating programs within Big Dogs.

Think of Big Dogs like going to the mall and to the food court. Big Dogs is the food court's manager, and the food court has a lot of different eateries to choose from. Good eateries will stay, and not-so-good ones will close down. The customer has the choice to purchase from one of the food places or many depending on the individual's tastes and what they perceive as value for money.

You were required to pay a monthly membership fee for each Big Dog program you joined. If you sponsor other people into the program, they become your downline members, and you would earn a commission from their monthly fee.

One of the lead-generating programs I joined was called Pro Money Mail by Brightstar Marketing Group Inc. Brightstar Marketing Group Inc. later became Business Opportunity Alliance Inc. and is now Gary Shawkey International Inc. (GSI). One thing I must tell you, things change on the Internet faster than the speed of light. Some things are here today and gone tomorrow. When I first started writing this book, I was a member of Pro Money Mail. Today, the name has been changed to PowereTools. I canceled my membership for all the other programs in Big Dogs except Pro Money Mail and Aureate Group Mailer.

I stayed with PowereTools because it was a quality program where the focus was target marketing, getting your ads directly in front of people who wanted to read them, and not by sending unsolicited email called *spam* to people who didn't request it.

Another reason I remained a member in this program was the leadership. The founder of Pro Money Mail/PowereTools is Gary Shawkey. From the first time I read Gary's personal emails that were sent to his members, I felt comfortable with his approach and he seemed to really care about his affiliates.

One really special and unheard-of thing that Gary did was this: he gave the members his direct hotline number. We could literally call him day or night. He was totally accessible. That spoke volumes to me. He had an email account that we could write to as well as a help desk. The emails actually got responded to, and the help desk was also efficient. These are two extremely important support features in an affiliate or network marketing program.

I quickly upgraded my membership in Pro Money Mail to *partner* status, then a few days later to *founder* status, so I'm a *senior partner founder* of Pro Money Mail. Well, actually, I'm a lifetime founder plus member of PowereTools. I can use PowereTools to market any program on the Internet.

In December 2001, I was invited through one of Gary's emails to join the BizOppAlliance business chat room in PalTalk. This business chat room was set up so members and interested parties could listen to Gary Shawkey on Mondays and Thursdays. Gary was a gifted promoter and a marketing guru, and he has spent twenty plus years in marketing. He shared this marketing experience through training in PalTalk.

When I started listening to Gary speak about marketing on the Internet, my mind was like a sponge, just sucking in all that knowledge. It was very interesting. He was always so upbeat and positive. After a two-hour meeting on a Monday night, I couldn't wait until Thursday night. Each week was better and better. It seemed like Gary always had new ideas. I was amazed that one person could concentrate on so many things at one time.

In the weekly meetings, there was a nucleus of people who always attended. You couldn't see them, but you knew their voices. There was Susan, the admin lady who spent countless hours in the room helping people. She would red-dot your name if you said something inappropriate. There was Georgia, the life of the party, always cheerful and encouraging. Georgia welcomed everyone to PalTalk and laid down the ground rules when the meeting was ready to begin. Her dedication to helping people was to be commended. Our dear Georgia suddenly passed away in March 2004. I think I can speak on behalf of all the members of GSI when I say this great lady is surely missed by all. I believe Susan and Georgia volunteered their service. Sometimes depending on the topic, there would be over 200 people in the room. After the meetings, Gary normally had a question and answer (Q&A) period where we could ask questions or just sit back and listen to others.

A big surprise came near the end of 2001. Gary told the members that we were going to make a CD. The name of the CD would be Biz Opp Gold. The concept was to create a CD that would be a complete business, giving users the resources to start and promote their work-at-home opportunities, hence the name BOIAB, Biz Opp in a Box. A group of people went to Orlando, Florida, to have a firewalk and training seminar with Gary, then off to another part of Florida to film an infomercial to market the CD. I couldn't go on that trip, but my heart was certainly there. Members chipped in and bought co-op shares that paid for the production of the CD and the infomercial. These members became part of the Team 2002. There was so much excitement amongst the members about the financial rewards that would start pouring in once the CD's started selling. The CD's would be put in major department stores and sold on the Internet and through infomercials. Everyone wanted to buy at least a few shares. I bought a few as I wanted a piece of the financial pie as well.

During 2002, Gary traveled to certain cities in the United States to train members to become coaches for Biz Opp Alliance. Again, I couldn't attend any of the seminars. By doing this, the workload got shared amongst several people. Many hands make light work and hopefully more profits are generated.

Gary announced a big surprise. This surprise would be an event called BLASST, Building Leadership and Super Success Training. Gary was going to take his twenty-one years of experience in marketing and have the biggest event ever. He and Dr. Sylvia Williams, the director of coaching for Gary Shawkey International, would train the coaches to become master coaches for the company. This event was held in Santa Clara, California, on February 6–10, 2003, and involved motivational speakers. Anyone who wanted to take their business and personal life to the next level needed to be at the event.

As I listened to Gary speak week after week about the event, I knew I had to be there. I wasn't a coach at that time. Gary made the members an offer to take a *free* thirty-day ecourse (electronic course on the Internet) to learn his marketing system, Shawkey's System. Shawkey's System taught you the correct way to market on the Internet. I took the course without hesitation. I was assigned a personal coach, Heather Lee, who helped me along the way. I was amazed how much I learned from that course. I had been doing some things right, but a lot of things wrong in my marketing efforts. That taught me another lesson, don't try and reinvent the wheel, do not be afraid to ask questions when you are not sure as someone has traveled that road before and can help you.

One night in PalTalk, when Gary was talking about the BLASST event, he said something about the importance of coaching which really caught my attention. You can probably think of a situation in your life where a coach has made a difference. After the meeting, I sent Dr. Sylvia Williams an email stating that I wanted to be a coach. I wanted to be on the team of coaches who taught people the correct way to market on the Internet.

There was some urgency on my part to do this right away. This was in December 2002. After getting a recommendation from my coach, Heather, I had to write a 3,500-word essay explaining Shawkey's System. Not a problem, I said to myself, so off I went to type my essay. When I finished, I did a word count, and it was just over one thousand words. I was shocked, but I was determined. I was determined to get that essay finished before leaving for vacation on December 22. I should have planned before jumping in, and the results could have been different. I revisited what I had written and decided to explain some of the points in more detail. I worked on it day by day, and I finished it. I sent it to Dr. Williams, and she sent me a confirmation that I was accepted into the coaching program. I was extremely happy and I really wanted to be a good coach and to make a difference.

About two weeks after I returned from vacation in January 2003, I got my first client. I was ecstatic. I couldn't wait to work with my client.

Now by this time, it's two weeks before the event in Santa Clara. I desperately wanted to go, and I kept telling my husband that I wanted to go. Gary said in a meeting one night, "I don't care what you have to do to get there, just get to the event." Sometimes words can be hypnotic; they move you into action. I knew I was going to face a few obstacles, so I prayed about it. I told God that I needed to be there, and I asked him to make a way if he thought I should go. God is so good. Everything fell into place. I came home from work one day and found my husband searching the Internet for ticket fares to Santa Clara. Are you kidding, my husband? I had to restrain my excitement. Seeing this, I knew God was making a way. I made all the arrangements without a hitch, and I was packed a week before the trip. I cannot tell you the excitement I had knowing I was going to attend the BLASST event. It's all I talked about.

There were going to be world-class speakers at the event. I heard Les Brown speak on the TV sometime ago, but I had not heard the others speak. I had purchased three books by Bob Burg, one of the speakers, and was reading *Endless Referrals* at the time. I couldn't wait to meet him in person. And I would finally get to meet Gary Shawkey, the man who had the vision to put the event together; the founder and CEO of Business Opportunity Alliance and Gary Shawkey International Network of Companies; the man who wrote the book *If I Can . . . Anybody Can*; the founder of Pro Money Mail, where I got started in his company. The man who created Biz Opp Gold CD, MLMDummies; the man with twenty-one years of marketing experience; the three-time *Guinness* book-of-records holder for firewalking; the man who displayed a heart of pure gold; the man with vision who had many new ventures to be launched at the event. How could I not be excited? I felt it would be money well spent and the benefits would be outstanding.

Hours of Pure Gold

I would also get to meet my PalTalk friends, my coach, and my client who were already like family to me. The rest you could say is living history.

"May you be truly inspired."

Tribute

You're probably wondering why I put a tribute in this section of the book. I do tend to do strange things at times.

In the introduction I mentioned some people who have influenced my life in one way or another and how the people of St. Monica's Church are so special to me.

When I began writing this book, I only told a handful of people and very few family members. One special family member that I told was my grandma Mary. I couldn't wait for the day it would be finished, and I would give her one of the first printed copies.

Giving her a copy would be accompanied by a big hug and thank you. Granny loved to read, and I know she would have read it from cover to cover and given me her honest opinion. I would let her know that her faith in God, her exemplary Christian lifestyle, her dedication to St. Monica's, her unselfish service to others, her love and care for her family, her perseverance in times of sickness and pain were the greatest influence in my life.

But this was not meant to be. The original last draft of the manuscript was completed on December 21, 2003. December 22 was my last visit with my grandmother, Mary Etheline Smith. She had come home from hospital as she wanted to be home for Christmas.

Kandi A. White

I left Bermuda to vacation in Florida on December 23 for twelve days. On December 30, 2003, granny passed to her eternal rest and is now in the company of God and his angels.

Granny, if you could see me now or know my thoughts, then you will know this tribute is for you. I will always treasure our chats and never forget all the wonderful things you did for your family and friends. You are surely missed.

As the refrain of the song says, "When we all get to heaven, what a day of rejoicing that will be! When we all see Jesus, we'll sing and shout the victory!"

So in my moments of sorrow and grief, I have faith in God's promises, and, Granny, I can't wait to see you again. I love you.

—Kandi

1

Journey to Santa Clara

I awoke at 4:00 a.m. Atlantic Standard Time on February 6, 2003, to get ready to travel to California. I was overjoyed as I was going to the BLASST event. Leaving Bermuda at 7:05 a.m., American Airlines flew me to the East Coast of the United States to JFK International Airport in New York City. The flight was full, but the ride was quite pleasant. I think I slept part of the way.

Arriving in New York, I was now in the Eastern Standard Time zone, so I gained an hour back. My layover was just over an hour before I boarded American Airlines to fly to San Francisco, California. That flight was full also, but I had a very nice man sitting next to me. He had been working in New York for some time and was excited to be going home to San Francisco where he would see his wife again. He really loved living in San Francisco and told me a lot about the city. It was my first time traveling there.

I told him about the BLASST event and how happy I was to be attending it. He didn't know much about Internet marketing but wished me much success.

Traveling to San Francisco took me from the East Coast to the West Coast of the United States, gaining another three hours. It was a beautiful day. On the East Coast I could see snow on the ground; looking out of the airplane windows I saw big patches of pure white snow. It was marvelous; I had never seen snow like that before. I watched a movie on the flight, read a book, and had a good lunch. The flight was five hours long, but it didn't seem that way. I'm not fond of long flights.

The last hour or so on the flight as I looked out of the window, I could see desert areas and mountains, craters, long winding dirt roads with no traffic. No houses or life in sight. I wondered what the road paths were for. Maybe it was my imagination. It was an absolutely beautiful sight to see, as far as I could see.

I arrived safely in San Francisco around 2:15 p.m. Pacific Standard Time then asked for directions to the shuttle pickup area. The curbside attendants that I spoke to never heard of "One Stop Shuttle" that I was expecting to pick me up and take me to Santa Clara.

After waiting for fifteen minutes and not seeing the shuttle, I decided to telephone the company. Inside the terminal was very crowded, and I couldn't find a phone. I ventured toward a booth that was collecting funds for charity. The attendant told me that if I gave a donation I could use his cell phone. A fair bribe I thought, so I gave him $5 and called One Stop Shuttle.

The man I spoke to did not speak English very well. He told me to wait at the curb at T4 and look out for the shuttle. It would be there in ten minutes. I never found T4, so obviously I didn't understand what he said. Ten minutes came and went, and I was getting a bit concerned. You see, I had a forty-five-minute ride to Santa Clara, had to check in at the hotel, call home, and get ready to go to the event.

Registration was from 3:00–5:45 p.m., and we were to be seated for a 6:00 p.m. start.

It was almost 3:00 p.m., and I didn't have any transportation. I asked a taxi driver how much it costs to go to Santa Clara. He kindly said $110.00, and I kindly said to myself, no, thank you. I went back to the curbside attendant and asked if there was a shuttle going to Santa Clara. He said there were two that I could take, and he called one of the companies for me. I had to wait another fifteen minutes, but I wasn't panicking as I still had enough time. Another lady came along who was taking the same shuttle to her destination.

The shuttle came around 3:30, and there was a man already on board. The lady and I boarded, and after a few minutes, we left the airport, and I felt somewhat relieved. Both passengers were getting out before me, so I knew it would take more than forty-five minutes. It took almost two hours. The lady was visiting from out of town and didn't quite know where she was going. All she had was a street name and number and knew her friend lived in the mountains. The driver wasn't familiar with the area either. I could see mountains all around, so I was totally lost. She telephoned her friend's house, but no one was at home, and she left a message.

The driver called the dispatcher, but he kept hearing the wrong street name, and we went on a tour of sorts. At first it was kind of funny but after a while became annoying. I was really trying to be patient. The man on board had traveled from the United Kingdom and had been awake a lot longer than I had. He suggested going to his house first, looking at a map, and finding the street the lady needed to get to. I was happy when the driver didn't take his suggestion. It was certainly an adventure, but I have to say the mountainside homes were beautiful as we drove around and around. We finally got the right directions from the dispatcher and found the street. We all cheered. We then dropped the man to his house and were on our way to Santa Clara.

I reached the hotel just before 5:30 p.m., checked in, called home, quickly freshened up, and gathered my notebook, wallet, camera, knapsack, and jacket. Off I went to the hotel lobby to find transportation to the Santa Clara Convention Center about one mile away.

To my surprise, the shuttle servicing the hotel to the convention center was "One Stop Shuttle." I had a brief chuckle. A lady was in the shuttle. She was going to the event also and had just arrived. Her name is Patti Kasper. Patti was the first person I met at the event. I asked the driver if he could leave right away as I was making time. We reached the convention center just before 6:00 p.m. and registered. Phew.

Registration consisted of verifying my name on a list and receiving a colored wristband that I had to wear all weekend. The wristband identified the seating area I was assigned to. People were still coming into the center after we arrived, and as I looked around everyone looked cheerful. Lots of chatter could be heard in small groups as we made our way to the meeting room. Patti and I both had executive seating, so we decided to sit next to each other. The doors were opened, and we entered the hall after receiving our master-coaching manual. Executive seating was a long row of tables behind the VIP round tables at the front. The room was huge, bigger than anything I had ever been in before for a seminar. It could have accommodated a few thousand people, but there was not that many in attendance. The big crowd that was expected didn't materialize.

Hours of Pure Gold

Patti sat to my left and Robert to my right. We sat slightly left of center stage within thirty feet of it. There were two very big screens on either side of the large stage, which showed the speakers in clear view and any taped footage that was shown. There was a podium on the stage, and the huge backdrop was a painting of a jungle. It was vivid and felt like being in another world. Sitting at the round VIP table right in front of me was Georgia, the voice of the party in PalTalk. I recognized her voice straight away. I was really happy she was sitting there. Once everyone was seated, it was lights, music, and action. A man appeared on the stage and BLASST is a reality.

2

BLASST Is a Reality

A man walked on the stage and started talking about his Internet experience of the last three years and how grateful he was to be part of Gary Shawkey International Group of Companies. You could tell this man was speaking from the heart. I later found out this was Jim Morrison, the administrative director for BizOpp4Kids, one of our programs. Jim spoke very highly of Gary Shawkey and introduced him to the stage.

Gary walked on the stage, and everyone applauded. I couldn't help but stare at him for a long time. I was absolutely amazed that he didn't, in my opinion, look anything like the person on the website picture that had been stamped in my memory for over a year. Don't get me wrong, he looked good, just different from the pictures.

I knew it was Gary, though, because that same caring voice was heard. The promoter voice was also heard. Gary welcomed everyone to the event and spoke to us for almost an hour. I could feel the rush of adrenaline throughout my body, and I was truly immersed in the moment of my good fortune, attending the event.

Gary said he would be talking to us about money a lot over the weekend. People say money isn't everything and money is evil. He doesn't disagree with this, but for those who don't have money it's very important. Gary isn't a psychologist but has spent many years trying to understand how some people can make a lot of money and why some can't. He promised us that the speakers would reveal why this is possible.

He then did something quite unexpected; he took out a wad of money from his pocket and started throwing $20 bills off the stage. He wasn't trying to brag or anything but only proving a point. Only one person left his seat and went to get the money; Gary said, "Some people get it and some don't when an opportunity is right there in front of everyone." Then he tried it again, and several people jumped from their seats and ran for the money. I'm sure you can think of circumstances in your life where you could kick yourself for not making a move when you had the opportunity.

Gary said the biggest thing he could give to everyone over the weekend was his time and everything he has learned over the last twenty-one years in how to be successful. The successful people are motivated, have intention, are mentored, have coaches and trainers. In other words, they take advantage of the resources that are available to them. They don't go the course alone or try to reinvent the wheel. Gary was a good talker and had big dreams and expectations for himself, his company, and his members. He spoke out loud his dreams and intentions, and he had the belief in achieving them. If things don't work out, he made changes and looked for other opportunities. That's a quality of a successful person.

Now I know that it's difficult sometimes to get motivated to achieving your dreams; I also have these moments. Sometimes we are searching and searching for answers that just don't seem to be there, and instead of being encouraged, we get discouraged. Sometimes when we are most encouraged, others only want to discourage us. I read something that said it's when we are at our lowest, at the brink of giving up, that's when we're open to unprecedented growth, because it takes dedication, faith, and even harder work to get back on our feet. I want to encourage you to take the small steps and not to give up when these circumstances occur. One of the motivational speakers, Mr. Jim Rohn, had a weekly ezine that I subscribed to. Week after week, I was more amazed with the wisdom and encouraging information Mr. Rohn shared with his subscribers. I invite you to review the motivational information by going to:

http://www.jimrohn.com
Copyright © Jim Rohn International.
All rights reserved worldwide.

In my own experiences, prayer is my relief when I'm at my lowest, and I firmly believe God will not give me more than I can handle or cope with. That voice inside of me gives me reassurance, and motivates me to carry on and not give up.

I like Isaiah 40:31: "But those who wait on the Lord shall renew their strength; they shall mount up with wings like eagles; they shall run and not be weary; they shall walk and not faint." What a wonderful promise of God, and God keeps his promises. I had an even deeper appreciation for that verse after the event and in writing this book.

Gary went over the schedule of events for the evening. After a session with Dr. Wayne Dyer, we would take a short trip to a stadium where the firewalking would take place. One thing I could sense from being in the room was how excited everyone was to be there. The atmosphere was electric.

Gary mentioned how he would have giveaways during the weekend. He introduced a wheel-of-fortune-type game that had dollar bills attached to certain numbers on the wheel. If you were picked to spin the wheel and land on some money, it was yours. Two gentlemen had a chance to spin the wheel. I think one of them won $20.

Gary reminded everyone about the chance each of us had to win the convertible car at the end of the weekend. Everyone clapped and cheered at that announcement.

Gary was dressed in jeans, a T-shirt, and a jacket. As he talked and paced the stage, he took off his jacket. It was a proud moment for him. He told everyone how he had lost sixty pounds since the Florida trip where the infomercial for the CD Biz Opp Gold was filmed. He considered himself still fat, but he was happy. Because of his diabetes problem, he started working out and taking Tiquando lessons. Everyone was so happy for Gary and gave him a thunderous round of applause.

Gary introduced his seven diamond coaches to the audience. I was training to be a master coach, so a diamond coach is quite an achievement. These were people who worked with Gary daily and which he had the utmost respect and gratitude. Each diamond coach was promised a seven-diamond ring as a gesture of appreciation. The team was called the GSI Xtreme 7 team.

These acts of giving by Gary Shawkey continued throughout the weekend, and I witnessed many of them.

Then Gary got to some serious talking with the audience. He talked about each of us individually and our involvement with his company. He asked us two questions.

The first question was "Why are you here?" and the second question was "What do you want to get out of this weekend?"

Gary told us to think about action and the power of action. He told us to think about our direction.

Shortly after, we took a fifteen-minute break, and when we returned, we listened to Dr. Wayne Dyer, the first invited motivational speaker of the weekend. During the short break, I began meeting other people. A very nice lady named Chris Morgan introduced herself to me, then she introduced me to her husband Ted. Chris and Ted live in Los Angeles, California. They were one of the first groups of coaches with Gary Shawkey International. I spent a lot of time with Chris and Ted over the weekend, sharing our experiences and our expectations from being coaches and members of Gary's companies. We were all so pleased to be at the event and very impressed with the quality of the speakers.

I also met Tina and John during the break. They were friends. Tina was a devoted mother of six who worked from home. John was not a member of Gary Shawkey International but was there to learn about the programs.

Someone told me during the break that my coach, Heather Lee, was looking for me. We met and gave each other a great, big hug. We finally put faces to voices. It was Heather's recommendation that gave me the opportunity to become a coach. In our PalTalk meetings on Mondays and Thursdays, Heather typed everything that Gary said for the hearing impaired. She sometimes anticipated what he would say and typed ahead. Gary often responded, "I didn't say it yet, Heather," and we all chuckled. We had a lot of fun in PalTalk. I'm fairly sure Heather also volunteered her time.

It was time to reenter the hall for the next master-coaching session.

3

An "Aha" Experience with Dr. Wayne W. Dyer

Our first motivational speaker was announced to the stage by Gary Shawkey. His name is Dr. Wayne Dyer. I had prepared myself to get totally motivated in relation to working my Internet businesses.

Yes, at the end of the session I was definitely motivated, but I also had a spiritual awakening and renewal that I didn't expect at all. This renewal came from being totally inspired by listening to Dr. Wayne Dyer. That was in 2003 and as I reflect on the event now, I can say God rescued me.

> *Dr. Wayne Dyer, called the "father of motivation" by his fans, is one of the most widely known and respected people in the field of self-empowerment. He became a well-known author with his best-selling book,* Your Erroneous Zones, *and has gone on to write many other self-help classics including,* There's a Spiritual

Solution to Every Problem and Staying on the Path, Pulling Your Own Strings, Everyday Wisdom, *and* You'll See It When You Believe It.

When Dr. Dyer entered the stage, he asked for a few moments to get set up and made a joke to the audience about the firewalking experience we would have later on that night. I think he was trying to scare us.

He lived in Maui and was working on a book that was a culmination of his life's work, and it would probably be his last book in that area. The book is called *The Power of Intention*. *The Power of Intention* is having an unbending desire in your heart, just like my unbending desire to be at the event and to write this book. *The Power of Intention* is now in bookstores; I purchased my copy.

Dr. Dyer told us about his childhood, being abandoned by his father, having two brothers and a loving mother who was always positive and labored to take care of her children. He told us how he lived in orphanages and how he was the richest kid in the orphanage. He was the only kid that had money all the time. It wasn't because he was special or more talented than the other kids were; he always knew in his heart the strangest secret. The strangest secret is "we become what we think about all day long." Our thoughts are the things that we use to create our reality. One thing Dr. Dyer mentioned frequently during his talk was for us to have an open mind. With an open mind, do you believe "you become what you think about all day long?" Yes, but you have to put some action toward it also.

I could really identify with his experience as a child although I never lived in an orphanage. One thing I could tell about Dr. Dyer is his deep love and gratitude for his mother who at the time of the event was eighty-seven years old and still bowled in three leagues. God bless her. Dr. Dyer was happily married and has eight children—six daughters and two sons.

He told us that everything in this universe is energy—every thought that we have. Energy is not good and bad, right and wrong, moral and immoral. There's only one source for everything, and that source is God. In the Bible, in the book of Genesis, it says "In the beginning God created heaven and earth and all that God created was good." He said, if you believe that, then where does that which is not good, such as evil, disorder, disease, disharmony, come from? It comes from our belief that we are separate from that source which we emanated. When we separate from our source, our energy moves away from God. We are said to have slow or low energy. When we shift that energy and return to the source and are in harmony with the source, those things which we call problems are impossible. Higher and faster energy converts lower and slower energy into love, peace, kindness, receptivity, and creativity. Again, with an open mind, this was a new way of looking at things. I found this very interesting, and I wanted to hear more.

Dr. Dyer wrote a book called *There's a Spiritual Solution to Every Problem*. At the event, my coach bought me a copy of this book, and she and Dr. Dyer signed it. When Heather presented the book to me, I cried. I was so grateful, and I will treasure it always. In the book, he explains in great detail being connected with God and the effect of fast and slow energy in relation to problem solving. It truly is an inspiring book. What would have taken me months to read took only weeks. Every spare moment I had, I was reading the book. I recommend you get a copy for your library.

Dr. Dyer spoke to us about being inspired in relation to our Internet marketing business. He mentioned something that Patanjali wrote three hundred years before Christ. Becoming inspired comes from "in spirit." When you are inspired by some great purpose, some extraordinary project, your consciousness expands in every direction, and you find yourself in a new, great, and wonderful world. Pantanjali said "dormant forces, faculties, and talents" come alive. You discover yourself to be a greater person by far than you ever thought before.

Now these words by Dr. Dyer caught my attention in a huge way; he said, "When you are in spirit, instead of being a human being having a spiritual experience, you become a spiritual being having a human experience." One that is eternal and can never die. That is so powerful, and I believe this to be true as God promises those who believe in him eternal life. Dr. Dyer told us that what he is saying may sound strange and weird, but he is speaking through experience. He knows in his heart that he is an infinite spiritual being in a temporal body. Sometimes it's not what a person says but how it is said that triggers an awakening, a moment when you say, "Aha." Yes, I had an "aha" moment.

When our thoughts are in harmony with God and we have a vision, we have the ability to attract anything we want in our lives. The greatest teacher who ever walked among us is Jesus. Jesus had very high energy. Jesus reminded us of this just by the things he did and his thoughts, like turning water into wine and raising people from the dead. Jesus said, "Even the least among you can do all that I have done and even greater things." Everyone has the capacity to do these things when we are in spirit.

Dr. Dyer knows this to be true. He always wanted to teach self-reliance, and he believes that's why he spent time in an orphanage. Living in an orphanage prepared him for what he would do later in life.

As I listened to Dr. Dyer, a very peaceful-looking man and whose voice was calm, unhurried, and so real, I couldn't believe that I had never heard of him before. I had to believe it was all part of God's plan for me. The impact of what he was saying affected the way I thought about my life, my career, my involvement with Gary Shawkey International, how I viewed other people, and most importantly my relationship with God.

I truly believe God used Dr. Dyer to awaken my mind and my soul. In an instant everything changed. I'm learning what my true purpose is in life, one of living for, loving, and serving God. This awakening helped me to put things in the right perspective. Some things that were really important when I went to the event went lower on the priority list, and some dropped off entirely. Giving my all to God and putting him first in everything and all relationships became number one. This walk with God and this relationship we are building is awesome and priceless. I continually pray and ask God to renew me, to remove my desires for worldly things. God hears our prayers and he is so faithful.

Dr. Dyer invited to the stage one of his daughters to sing for us who is also another one of his heroes. Her name is Skye Dyer, and she has been singing from a very early age with a burning desire. Don't you just love that name *Skye*? The first song Skye sang was called "Call the Man." As she was singing, Dr. Dyer was looking at her with total admiration, and you could see how proud he was of her and his love for her.

The song "Call the Man," meant this to me: whenever we need love or care or help, we should call on the name of Jesus. God will make all things clear when we call on Jesus' name. When we don't have the answers and are afraid, call on Jesus, rely on him. Know that all things come together for good for those who love the Lord.

In this world of chaos and fear, God is always there for us. When we feel at our lowest moments, when we've done all that we can do about a troubling situation, when we don't know what to do next, we should close our eyes and call on Jesus as he's always there and can mend anything. We don't have to travel this road alone. If God can bring you to it, he certainly can bring you through it.

Skye's voice was angelic, so pure, and so caring. I instantly became a fan. We were told that we could purchase her just-released CD after the session out in the foyer. The CD is called "This Skye Has No Limits." I decided to buy two CDs, one for a special friend.

Dr. Dyer told us, "Don't die with your music still in you." If you have a vision, a burning desire, don't wait until you are old and weary; get on with it now. All of us were intended here by a source. Everything comes from that source, and everything we ever need was created in the moment of our conception.

If you could reach into my mind, you would find an endless stream of ideas and dreams. Without *dreams* there is no *reality*. There is so much work to be done in God's kingdom. Forever will I praise him and humbly serve him. I urge each person reading this book to embrace his/her dreams and to start working on them. Don't go to your grave with them unfulfilled; better yet, don't wait another month, day, or minute. Begin now, and by just beginning, you will feel empowered to go on. When times get hard or things are not quite going your way, step back, reflect, rest, but don't let the dream die.

Each of us has a burning desire. We become what we think about. Our thoughts are a magic elixir. In the Old Testament of the Bible, it says, "As a man thinketh, so is he."

We are the product of our thoughts, and our thoughts are very powerful.

He reminded us of obstacles that keep us from fulfilling our intentions. One obstacle is when we think of what is missing from our lives, like money, good health, relationships, ideal weight, and many other things; the energy attracted back to us can only be what it missing. In order to change, we have to shift the emphasis to what we intend to have or be. Sounds so simple and easy, doesn't it? Dr. Dyer talked about meditating and spoke about two CDs he developed on the subject of meditating. The CDs are called "Meditations for Manifesting" and "Getting in the Gap." "Meditations for Manifesting" is based on the repetition of the sound *ah* and attracting whatever you need in your life to show up. The repetition of the sound *ah* connects us to our source where miracles can be performed. He stressed how powerful meditating is and how it works for him. Dr. Dyer teaches meditation and gives all profits to charity. He was truly speaking from the heart.

I never gave much thought to meditating, but I certainly had the desire to look into it from a curious perspective. I liked how Dr. Dyer referenced the Bible passages as examples in his teaching. After the session, I purchased both CDs, and at the time of writing, I can honestly say it was a great decision. I start and end each day meditating with Dr. Dyer, and my life is richly blessed from the experience. I certainly have seen manifesting in my life. I am more focused, more loving and kind, more organized. Meditating on God's word is first and foremost. God is truth and his word is truth. Every time I meditate on God's word I learn more about him and his love for us. My heart, soul, and mind longs to read about his mighty acts and his compassion for his people. Meditation allows me to refuel emotionally, especially after a long, hard day and when tasks seem overwhelming as they sometimes do. Meditating allows me to go away and relax in the presence of God and listen to him. So much has changed. Don't take my word for it, try meditation for yourself.

Dr. Dyer wanted to demonstrate the power of energy to the audience. Every thought that we have is energy. Everything in the universe is energy. Our thoughts will either strengthen or weaken us depending on what they are at any given moment. He called two people from the audience to help demonstrate the power of energy. Lynda LaCour was his volunteer, and Glen was his assistant. Once again, have an open mind.

Dr. Dyer asked Lynda to honestly state her name. He told us that our bodies can only respond to truth and be strengthened; any thought that we have that is not truthful will weaken us.

Lynda was asked to extend her right arm and to make a fist as she repeated her name truthfully and to hold on to that thought. As she did, Dr. Dyer tried to press down on her arm with lots of pressure. He was unable to press her arm down.

He then told her to tell a lie, and she would be forgiven when he asks her name. As she held out her right arm again making a fist and said her name untruthfully, Dr. Dyer easily pressed her arm down. The body can only react to truth. Now someone can say that this was a trick or he paid her off, but I don't think so. It looked genuine.

Dr. Dyer demonstrated and explained the power of energy with other examples: thoughts of love and shame, listening to good and degrading music, holding Skye's uplifting CD and holding an envelope with an artificial substance and thinking of someone who symbolizes high spiritual principles and someone who is evil.

Hours of Pure Gold

Energy is in everything. In order to overcome instances when we exhibit lower energy, we have to bring higher energy into our presence. Dr. Dyer reminded us of the famous prayer of St. Francis of Assisi. This prayer tells us what to do, what to think, how to bring this higher energy into our presence.

A long time ago, someone kindly gave me a copy of that prayer on a small piece of stained glass, which I kept on my desk at work. It was visible to me five days a week. It's absolutely beautiful, and I'm very thankful for it.

The prayer goes like this:

> **Lord** make me an instrument of thy peace,
> Where there is hatred let me sow love;
> Where there is injury, pardon;
> Where there is doubt, faith;
> Where there is despair, hope;
> Where there is darkness, light; and
> Where there is sadness, joy.
> O Divine Master,
> Grant that I may not so much
> Seek to be consoled as to console;
> To be understood as to understand;
> To be loved as to love;
> For it is in giving that we receive;
> It is in pardoning that we are pardoned;
> And it is in dying that we are born to eternal life.
>
> St. Francis of Assisi

I finished reading the book that my coach, Heather, gave me at the event written by Dr. Dyer, *There's a Spiritual Solution to Every Problem*. In the book, Dr. Dyer writes about this very inspiring prayer and explains in great detail how it brings higher and faster energy to anyone who carries out these acts.

Dr. Dyer read some of the principles that Mother Teresa lived by. As you know, Mother Teresa gave her life to help others and commissioned everyone to be kind and loving. I can only imagine the energy she generated and just being in her presence made remarkable differences to people's lives.

Before closing for the evening, Dr. Dyer asked Skye to sing us another song, one of his all-time favorites, and he told us that the words were very inspirational. The song Skye sang was "It's in Every One of Us." The song was beautiful. It tells us to find our heart, open our eyes, that we can have and know everything without ever knowing how or why. God's greatness surpasses all understanding.

Have you ever witnessed a miracle or had a miracle in your own life? These are times when we can't explain why it occurred but we know that God was in control. God is the creator and founder of miracles. Open your heart and your mind to receive yours by staying close to God.

Dr. Dyer reminded us that we all emanated from the same source, and everyone has within them the power and ability to leave their egos behind and to bring this higher source to what we call problems or shortages and instantly rectify them. That's a very powerful statement for someone to make. My mind and my heart were yearning for more of his teaching. I was so jazzed and excited. I couldn't wait to hear him speak again. I am eternally grateful to God for bringing Dr. Dyer and Skye into my presence.

Dr. Dyer said something that I will never take for granted ever again. He said, "If you know who walks beside you every place you go, you will have no fear." Shouldn't we be mindful that when we look to God and walk with him that we don't have to let the small and unimportant concerns hold us down?

> Motivation, spiritual awakening, peace, joy, abundance, gratitude—yes, I felt them all.

4

I'm Going to Firewalk

After listening to Dr. Dyer, we left the convention center and boarded buses that took us to a sports arena a few miles away. When we arrived, there were fields sectioned off, and people were playing various sports. On one of the fields, I could see flames rising in the air, and everyone was naturally drawn to it. This is where the preparation for the firewalk was taking place by personally trained instructors of Gary Shawkey. I remember going quite near a great big bonfire that was throwing off some serious heat. People were asking, "Where are the marshmallows?" Going to the fire, we passed a huge mound of unburnt firewood. It must have been ten to fifteen feet high. For a quick moment, I thought how on earth were they going to burn all that firewood. I convinced myself that the fire was going to burn down quite a bit more before I was supposed to walk on it. I hadn't a clue about firewalking or the preparation. All I knew is that Gary Shawkey was the *Guiness* three-time world-record holder who had successfully walked many people across the hot coals. Hot coals of 1,800 degrees Fahrenheit. Many of our coaches had already firewalked in Orlando, Florida the year before and survived, so my chances were pretty good too.

Gary asked us all to move to a seated area where he would begin coaching us about firewalking. He explained that the coals are hot and that we could get burnt, but if we followed his instructions, we could successfully do it like the other 1,500 people he had coached.

Gary reminded us that after we successfully do the firewalk, we will have no fear doing anything ever again that is challenging in our lives. Have you ever done something really challenging outside of your comfort zone? That sounded great to me, but I will never bungee jump. Everyone was so excited, and mostly everyone around me was so psyched and geared up to get going.

We were handed some indemnity forms, and we had to read a few pages of questions and statements and agree by signing our initials and our name. No one was allowed to firewalk without signing the form. It was for Gary's protection and to certify that we were not forced but were taking the risk on our own accord.

Do you know that people can die firewalking? Gary told us that, and at that point I decided to really pay attention to the instructions. Death was not part of the agenda for the weekend. I was having the time of my life.

Gary said, "If you walk up to the coals, then look down, then step on them, you will get burnt, no doubt about it." He reminded us of Dr. Dyer's teaching that whatever we focus on with our minds we will get. He also reminded us to be careful what we wish for as we can sometimes focus on the wrong things. Isn't that the truth!

He said that firewalking is no big deal, no trickery involved. To be successful, we have to focus beyond the fire, focus on already completing it and celebrating. He said to think about something we want to accomplish or a fear we want to get rid of. See the accomplishment in our minds, confront the fear. He reminded us that our fears are created by BS—that is our belief systems—and we can control our minds to believe that fear really exists or that we can overcome fear.

I remember feeling very hungry; some people bought food from the snack bar. Chris offered me some nachos, which I gladly accepted. A cup of tea is what I was really craving.

Gary said that firewalking is a metaphor to help us focus on a purpose. As a coach for GSI, we must be focused and empowered, firstly to assist ourselves, and secondly to empower our clients. He told us to use the word *yes* as an anchor, and when *yes* is repeated over and over, it helps us to empower ourselves. We were asked to raise our hand, grab the energy from the air, make a fist, and pull down repeating *yes* as we pulled. *Yes* is a strong, powerful word. Saying *yes* sets our minds to accomplish our desires and will work for us every time.

As a group, we can accomplish something together by working together. We will succeed if we are there for each other. Gary said we were a close-knit group of people. I felt that as well. When coaching, there will be difficult times, but if we use the information that we learn or have been taught by one another, we can get through the difficult times. Isn't it true in life that teamwork makes the load lighter, and we often have to depend on others for help during difficult times? I can attest that knowing and spending time with God allows me to have peace even through personal storms. God is always there and available to protect and care for us.

Gary said that he would be there to coach us and to demonstrate for us how to firewalk. After some more coaching and affirming from Gary, we moved to the area where fifteen-foot fire beds were being spread with hot, flaming coals. The coals were scooped from wheelbarrows and spread out with shovels. You could hear the shovels hitting the coals as they were laid out.

In the background, there was a group of bongos drummers playing an African kind of beat. It was very stimulating and helped to add to the excitement. People quickly rolled up their trousers, took off their shoes, and walked across the hot coals, chanting "yes, yes, yes..." until they reached the other side. I just followed them; I don't remember seeing Gary do the walk, and I'm not sure if he did or not. People were simply jazzed, focused, and ready. As people walked across, more hot coals were spread out, and the drummers raised the beat. The atmosphere was electrifying. I started to walk across, chanting, and when I got midway across, for a split second, I lost focus, and yes, I felt the heat. I had to do it a second time where I remained focused the whole way across, chanting "yes, yes, yes." I was met and hugged at the finish line by Eileen Egleton, one of the master firewalkers that helped prepare the coals. It was such an accomplishment. I was quite proud.

Some people walked across very slowly, others kept a quick pace, and others danced with a partner back and forth across the hot coals. There were people onlooking, and I sometimes wonder what they must have been thinking. We were having so much fun. This part of the event was also being filmed by TVWorldwide.com, and people were taking personal pictures as well. Everyone was hugging and singing and clapping and dancing and chanting "yes, yes, yes."

I was extremely proud to accomplish the firewalk, and I know I can do anything I set my mind to. When I was growing up, I lived below a nightclub where my mom worked as a cashier. Over the years, I would go and see the calypso show at the club. There was a guy named Marishow who danced on broken glass and on burning glass. I've seen the show a hundred times at least, and I was always amazed how he did not get cut or burned. I now understand how he did it. He used to have a warm-up dance, and I'm certain that's when he was preparing his mind to focus on completing this death-defying act.

Again, the firewalk was used as a metaphor to focus on a specific purpose. It was an act of faith in God, in Gary, in myself when I walked across the hot coals. I was focusing on being a successful coach and Internet marketer and making a difference.

5

Why Am I Here—
It's More Than Lunch!

After the firewalk was finished and we went back to the hotel, I was so hungry and craving for a cup of hot tea. It was late at night, and all the restaurants in the hotel were closed. Not being familiar with the area, I knew I had to wait until the next day to get something to eat.

I prepared for bed and tucked myself in around 1:30 a.m. Now, back in Bermuda, where I started out the day before it was 5:30 a.m. I had been awake for twenty-five and a half hours.

I remember being tired but excited and jazzed at the same time. I woke at 4:30 a.m. and could not go back to sleep. All sorts of thoughts were running through my head. I was so thankful to be there and so happy.

I decided to write a personal letter to Gary Shawkey answering his question "Why are you here?" After listening to Dr. Dyer's presentation the night before, I explained to Gary that I thanked God who made it all possible for me to be there. It was no coincidence that I felt totally connected to my source and that God was revealing more of his plan for my life. The experience I was having was just like fitting together pieces to a puzzle perfectly. I wrote a lot of things in that letter to Gary from the beginning of my involvement with his company to the present time. I remember being so excited that I couldn't write fast enough.

I told Gary that it was no coincidence that Dr. Dyer, a man I had never heard of before, was the first speaker and the impact he had on my life. Dr. Dyer set the stage for my mind to be open and receptive during the weekend. He helped prepare me mentally to do the firewalk. I simply couldn't wait to hear Dr. Dyer speak again.

I knew that being involved in GSI and training to be a master coach for the company was a good decision. I knew that the enjoyment and the rewards would far surpass my expectations.

After I finished the letter, I wrote another copy that was neater. I wasn't sure when I would give it to Gary, but I knew I would.

I got dressed and went down to the restaurant to have breakfast. By this time I was famished. I had a pancake breakfast. They were expensive pancakes but delicious and with them a cup of hot tea. I was set for the day. All was in order. Whilst eating breakfast, I couldn't help but look around and wonder if some of the people were also going to the event. I was wondering if they were as happy as I was.

The first session for Friday, February 7, 2003, was scheduled to begin at 9:00 a.m. I shared a taxi with two other people who were waiting out front of the hotel.

After the morning session and just before lunch, I gave Gary the letter and told him everything was fantastic.

I went to look for my client, Richard Guarnieri, to see if we could have our first face-to-face meeting over some lunch. Someone pointed Richard out to me. He was manning a booth for Gary in another room. I introduced myself to him, and we began talking. We were glad to finally meet one another. As we were talking, getting to know each other, a very stately man approached me wearing a black suit. He introduced himself as Richard Fields, head of security for Gary Shawkey International, and asked if I was Kandi White. I knew I hadn't done anything wrong, so what could security possibly want with me. I answered yes with a bit of hesitation.

Mr. Fields stated that Gary Shawkey would like to invite me to the speaker's lunch and all the meals with the speakers. I was lost for words but gladly accepted the invitation. Words cannot explain how thankful and overjoyed I was. The speaker's meals were sold separately from the event tickets. There were seven occasions over the weekend to do this. Being prudent with my spending, I had bought three tickets before coming to the event. The first would have been dinner on Friday night with Les Brown and Gary Shawkey.

I went upstairs to the room where lunch was being served, and I was feeling very humbled. I wasn't sure what to say to Gary. I went to Gary's table, shook his hand, and said, "Thank you, Gary."

I wasn't even hungry as I was so excited. Soon after I sat down, in walked Dr. Dyer, and the room was jubilant. I got to meet him personally, and I took pictures with him. I will treasure these moments forever. Being in his presence, I could just feel the positive energy in the room. It was an absolutely awesome experience. Dr. Dyer moved from table to table and chatted with everyone. I told him how much I enjoyed listening to him and that it was really affecting me in a special way. I told him that I couldn't understand why I had not heard of him before. He definitely brought a new meaning to spirituality than I had ever experienced. Another lady, Kathy, felt the same way as I did. We both had an "aha" moment.

Have you ever had the desire to meet a particular person and can only dream how great that would be? That's how I felt—so blessed. Being invited to the meals was a priceless experience. Each speaker had their own unique style and wonderful personalities. I am so grateful for the opportunity to sit, chat, and dine with these remarkable people. I will never forget the kindness and generosity that Gary displayed. Thanks again, Gary.

I have to tell you once again that God is so good. He only wants the best for us and promises to give us the desires of our hearts. BLASST changed my life and my life focus. Believe me when I tell you God is helping me to pen these pages and the emptiness, the chasing after riches for self gain is gone. God has closed all the gaps and fills every void in my life. He wants to do the same for you. Will you give him a chance?

It only gets better.

6

Master Coaching with Gary Shawkey and Dr. Sylvia Williams

Dr. Sylvia Williams, Ed.D, CED, was the chief executive coach for Gary Shawkey International, Inc. She was responsible for providing the training and tools to all the coaches involved in BizOpp Coaches, an online personal and marketing coaching system developed by Gary Shawkey. Sylvia lived in Sacramento, California, and had been involved in sales and marketing for nearly twenty-five years and had been marketing on the Internet for over four years. Sylvia holds a doctorate degree in education that she draws heavily upon as she teaches the coaches. She believes very strongly that anyone can make a good income on the

Internet if they are simply taught how to follow a system that works. Sylvia believes that Gary Shawkey has the only comprehensive step-by-step system for success on the Internet.

Gary spoke to us about the goals we set. He stressed the importance of making a list of goals and ticking them off as they are accomplished. It doesn't matter if they are accomplished quickly or years later. Writing them down and reviewing them is most important.

Dr. Williams, Sylvia as we call her, talked to us about being a master coach and what it really means. The dictionary meaning of a coach is (1) a four-wheeled horse-drawn carriage, and (2) a vehicle that moves a person from here to where they want to go. As a coach for Gary Shawkey International, I am a vehicle to take people through the coaching course to get them grounded in the right fundamentals of Internet marketing. Through this experience, I can be a catalyst for making their dreams come true.

Coaching is a partnership where the coach and client work together to achieve their purpose. Sylvia asked each person to think about writing their own mission statement and explained the importance of having a mission statement.

Each person in the audience and those listening over the Internet were asked to think about what's important to each of us and to write these things down. I like the saying "Don't think them, ink them."

We reviewed the requirements to become a master coach for Gary Shawkey International. These requirements can be summarized as follows:

1. First become a client – that means you must go through the free *thirty-day ecourse*. Before beginning the ecourse, you can choose a personal coach or get one assigned to you. The personal coach will assist with any questions with the ecourse and is there to assist and lend support. The ecourse is designed to teach the correct way of marketing on the Internet.
2. Become a coach yourself. To do that you have to write a 3,500-word essay explaining Shawkey's Internet marketing system. You must get a recommendation from your personal coach. You must really care about your clients and want to make a difference in their lives.
3. You must attend a training seminar with Gary Shawkey, like the BLASST event. You must attend a firewalking event but not necessarily have to participate in the walk.

You must be willing to put in the time and be dedicated with desire and commitment to the program.

Sylvia shared with us some qualities of a master coach. Master coaches:

- have strong sense of love for oneself
- have strong sense of purpose and mission
- have desire to help
- are willing to study and work at coaching
- are confident
- are willing to learn and become better
- are authentic, real, and have strong convictions and values
- listen deeply to clients
- create trust with clients
- convey realistic expectations with clients

Kandi A. White

Coaching is a very serious commitment, and I am willing to put my all into it. My business responsibilities, parental responsibilities, Leadership responsibilities, and community responsibilities all have various aspects of coaching. Sometimes we just need that extra bit of guidance to be more effective in what we do.

7

The Fullness of Truth with Dr. Wayne W. Dyer

Gary introduced Dr. Dyer and said we were privileged to have him address us again. I echoed those sentiments especially after having my mind and soul awakened the day before.

Dr. Dyer previously spoke to us about the power of the mind and gave us a demonstration of that power with Lynda LaCour. What he told us was a lead up to what we would hear in this session. He reminded us that higher and faster energy dissolves or nullifies lower and slower energy; for example, bringing light into a dark room removes the darkness.

He strongly advised us to read a book by David R. Hawkins called *Power vs. Force: The Hidden Determinants of Human Behavior.*

Dr. Dyer said when reading we need to willingly suspend our disbelief that every thought we have has an impact on anyone we encounter. If we are steadfast in abstaining from a harmful thought of others, all living creatures will cease to feel enmity in our presence. I purchased the book and promised to read it with an open mind and to formulate my own opinion. I could only read small sections at a time, and I am not ready to give an opinion. It's not your normal novel; it's quite intense and technical. While listening to Dr. Dyer speak about this subject, I did find the concept interesting at least to research.

After years of study, Hawkins used kinesiology to make millions of calibrations of human consciousness that follows a logarithmic progression from 0 to 1,000.

It is said that 87 percent of people in the universe calibrate below 200. St. Francis of Assisi calibrated at 900. Mother Teresa calibrated at 600. When you're in the presence of a high calibrator, you feel their presence as it radiates from them. In the presence of Jesus, your level of consciousness would automatically be raised. No one could continue to suffer in the presence of Jesus who calibrated at 1,000. Everything in the universe is energy and is impacted by the scale at which we calibrate. We can all raise our level of energy by our thoughts and by what we put in our bodies.

Dr. Dyer spoke of his own struggles with addictions in his life with drugs, caffeines, and nicotines, and how he overcame them. He stated that every time you put substances in your body that weakens you, you become separated from your source—God. You weaken your temple.

How can we keep from using force to create war? Force stems from anger and hatred and having a low energy, below 200. To avoid war, you must make an attempt to remove the hatred by bringing a higher energy of love and converting the hatred to love.

Would you say to a crying baby at 2:00 a.m. to stop crying and leave it unattended, or instead would you show love by breast-feeding or giving the baby a bottle? When the World Trade Center was hit on September 11, 2001, the first instinct of many people was to be kind and compassionate. Firefighters, police, medical staff, and volunteers worked around the clock. People donated blood without hesitation. Wouldn't we live in a remarkably loving world if more people acted this way on a daily basis? Dr. Dyer reminds us that we must come up with another way other than force to solve our disputes. My friends continue to pray for peace, and my prayer for each of you is to experience the peace that passes all understanding. Personally, this peace only comes from my relationship with God, knowing that Jesus died for my sins and your sins, and that the Holy Spirit dwells in my heart. There is no love greater than God's love. We must show love to others even when it is difficult, to begin breaking down the barriers of hatred and war.

Those who calibrate between 200 and 300 shift away from force and have higher levels of consciousness and can make a difference or impact to people around them by showing love and peace. These people make you feel better about yourself. You feel energized, awakened, and feel like everything is going to work out for the best. The opposite is true of being in the presence of those who calibrate below 200. Just from being in their presence, you feel drained and weakened. There is no hope, and everything is doom and gloom. It is said that one person who calibrates at 700 can counterbalance seventy million individuals who calibrate below 200. Is this really true? If it is, it's truly astonishing.

If you are hateful with someone who is hateful with you, it will bring you down, but if you learn something different, you can be lifted up. The prayer of St. Francis says, "Where there is hatred, let me sow love." Love nullifies hate. As Dr. Dyer said, "We must willingly suspend our disbelief." Carry something positive around that can make an impact and transfer higher energy.

Dr. Dyer invited Skye to sing for us the "Prayer of St. Francis." Just hearing the words of the song when we are struggling or feeling down or sad can really transform our energy. I was already feeling jovial just for being at the BLASST event, and I'm absolutely certain my calibration level rose a few notches. Dr. Dyer said we must make a conscious decision to "no longer invite" the lower energies into our lives. That implies that we have a choice; we are each in control.

In the moment of our conception, a tiny, microscopic dot was everything that we were destined to become as a human being—from the height we would become to the color of our hair and eyes. Look at the dot and ask yourself where the dot came from that began you. The source of the dot is creative, kind, loving, and beautiful. It is *love*, it is *God*. "Be still and know that I am God." The universal field from which we emanated is beautiful and can only bring beauty. Beauty is truth, and truth is beauty. This love, beauty, and truth is endlessly abundant. To understand this, you must be in the same field as it is, or simply said, "have a relationship with God."

Skye sang for us once again, and this time she sang a favorite and popular hymn, "Amazing Grace." This hymn always sends a shiver through my body. It speaks to my inner being. Yes, a wretch like me was once lost, but now I'm found, was blind to the truth, but now I see. Dr. Dyer explained how the song was created when John Newton was carrying slaves on a boat from Africa to England. They came upon a storm, and Mr. Newton realized what he was doing was against the laws of the universe. After the storm was over, he turned his ship around and released the slaves. He went back to England and became a speaker against slavery. This could only have been an act of God speaking to John's heart for which he did a complete about-face. God also speaks to you and me; let us be receptive to his voice and follow the path he has set out for us. Not my will, God, but your will be done. Will it be easy? Probably not. Will it be fulfilling? Definitely yes.

How easy is it for us to go out into the world and talk of God's love? It's easy when we are in the company of believers, and more difficult in the company of nonbelievers. It's not easy; it's like sending lambs into a pack of wolves. Don't give up, my friends. Pray that our lives will be lived in a manner pleasing to God and that people will see his love through us.

Dr. Dyer again spoke about meditation and that when we meditate, we grow spiritually, we get to know the meaning of our lives. We grow because we are in total silence and God's only voice is silence.

There is just no way I can give justification to the spiritual awakening or to Dr. Dyer for his compelling teaching. He is truly a remarkable human being who walks in the spirit of God. I thank God that he brought him into my presence. I just wish everyone in the entire universe could hear his teachings.

I've heard it said, "when the student is ready, the teacher shows up". I learned so much from Dr. Dyer and I had this hunger to learn so much more about the God I love. My prayers to attend the BLASST event were answered and I can just imagine the smile on God's face when he thought about what was in store for me.

8

Fulfill Your Dreams with Les Brown and . . . Never Give Up with Denice Young

As a renowned public speaker, author, and television personality, Les Brown has risen to national prominence by delivering a high-energy message that tells people how to shake off mediocrity and live up to their greatness. It is a message Les Brown has learned from his own life and one he is helping others apply to their lives.

Les Brown is not only an internationally recognized speaker and CEO of Les Brown Unlimited, Inc., he is also the author of the highly acclaimed and successful book, Live Your Dreams, and former host of The Les Brown Show, a

Hours of Pure Gold

nationally syndicated daily television talk show which focused on solutions rather than problems.

Before our session with Les Brown, I had the privilege of meeting him during dinner. He came and sat at our table for a few minutes as he was making his rounds, greeting and talking to people. Les has a very serious and quiet side to his personality, which I was able to discern from speaking with him. He asked us questions about the Internet marketing business, about our expectations and how we were going to be successful at it. I knew that to be successful I should heed the advice of all the speakers and make some changes. I just couldn't believe my good fortune sitting opposite this larger-than-life, successful individual. I wanted to know more about him and how he got to where he is today.

Let me tell you a secret, the stage transforms Les Brown into an extremely lively and comical individual. He is full of life and laughter. I thoroughly enjoyed listening to Les speak. It's such a pleasure watching a person enjoying their profession.

Les also had his personal story and struggles growing up as a young boy. The struggles he had made him determined to succeed in life. He told us, "Don't let anyone tell you that you are a failure and can't accomplish your desires." Each speaker reminded us of this in their own special way, and I firmly agree with them.

You can never learn too much. Les is very excited about the commitment GSI has made to teaching and coaching its members. It's not only a commitment of Gary but of the members as well. We must constantly raise the bar on ourselves. He told us that as coaches we need to expand, or we will be expendable. This is not a new revelation; teachers like Gary, Dr. Dyer, and Jim Rohn have already told us this fact. This is true for whatever we do in life. Let's encourage our children, let them encourage their friends. Let's not become complacent but to "raise the bar."

Les is so funny; he said, "Money ain't important, but it's right up there with oxygen," and, "Money can't buy you happiness, but it's a good down payment." I pray that the proceeds from *Hours of Pure Gold* would create some happiness for those who have lost hope and that God's spirit will move amongst them, wake them up so that they will become encouraged, not discouraged. The society in which they live will be better for it. This would be a miracle.

Les asked us a question and gave us the answer: "What do you get out of life?" He said, "You don't get in life what you want, you get in life what you are." As you look at your dreams, you must sell yourself on them every day, meditate on them. There's that "meditate" word again, I was enjoying this. In order to do something you've never done, you've got to be someone you've never been. With power, feeling, and conviction, it's possible to achieve your dreams and desires. We must sell ourselves on our ability to teach someone, or to help someone who's having problems. We must not give up on our dreams when someone criticizes us, we must carry on. We've failed once we've given up.

Les had a goal of reducing the number of women who die from breast cancer and the number of men who die from prostate cancer by encouraging them to get tested.

Through God's grace and mercy, his life was changed because of people who coached him. Do not let someone's bad opinion of you make you become someone you are not. Find someone who can encourage you. Encouragement helps to build self-esteem and helps you through the difficult times. There will be difficult times, it's a fact of life. It's in the difficult times that God can turn us around and produce miracles in our lives. Look at some of the people in the Bible who had real life experiences. Look at David and Paul and how God transformed their lives.

Les had a great love for his mother and wanted to make her proud. She was everything to him because of her love for him and how she worked hard for her children as a single mom. He had a goal to take care of her, and he excelled and did just that.

I've had a chance since the event to ponder many of these phrases that Les said and to make some adjustments to the way I do things. I can think of many projects I've started over the years and not completed. I can also think of achievements that I've made and sacrifices along the way. I knew without a doubt that I would finish *Hours of Pure Gold* and share it with others. I know without a doubt that the information is valuable and can help someone. I could have quit many times when obstacles got in the way, but I remained focused. I focused and imagined the end in sight, or maybe it's a new beginning of a new and wonderful experience. I'm open to all possibilities. I thank God for being in the driver's seat and steering my path.

I like coaching, and I want to be a coach that makes a difference, has integrity, and is willing to help her clients. I have dreams and expectations, and the first step to succeeding is believing, finding a mentor, doing the things that other successful people do.

Les said, "Hold yourself to high standards." What will set you apart from others? As coaches, we gain a reputation, and he asked us to think about what type of reputation we will have in our coaching relationships. Will we be knowledgeable, good listeners, a person of integrity, patient, committed, or otherwise?

He advised each person to "live full and die empty." He talked of a friend named Boo who died but never wrote the cookbook he had intended. He said one of the wealthiest places on the planet is the cemetery. There you will find talented and gifted people who never had the chance to share their gifts. Things that cause people to die full are fear of success, fear of failure, not feeling good enough, not enough education. We must be willing to do the things today others won't do in order to have the things tomorrow others won't have. Les' quotes were so thought provoking. He had such great stage presence, and he also spoke from the heart and from experience. Are you willing to live full? I am.

He advised us as coaches to make discipline a force in our lives. He had a coach, Mr. Washington, that helped him change his view of himself. Now this is powerful, Les said, "Leap and grow your wings on the way down." He said, "Faith is finding answers in the heart. Make your move before you're ready and to walk by faith and not by sight. If you have something you want to accomplish, get started and learn along the way. Don't wait until everything is perfect, it may never be." In our own lives, when God calls us to fulfill a purpose, he doesn't always give us the blueprint. We must have faith and believe in God's mighty power to complete the task. God doesn't fail.

Les took a short break so that we could listen to a lady he was coaching. He introduced to us the dynamic Denice Young.

From the first few sentences Denice spoke, I knew she was a lady with a message and that I'd better pay attention. Denice was smartly dressed, had a confident, clear voice, and liked to pace the stage in a dancelike fashion. Denice also attended the dinner with Les Brown, and she is a good listener. She named some of the people she met during the meal and spoke of their involvement with coaching. She appeared to do this from memory, as she had no notes in front of her. I was very impressed.

She expressed that we have the power to fulfill our dreams. We must make our own decisions, or life will decide for us. It's only those who can see the invisible who can do the impossible. To do this, we have to guard our mind and our life as we have to make the same decision tomorrow. Work our talents, be disciplined, and move according to purpose. She told us to ask ourselves, "Why am I here and where am I going?" We have to live life on purpose, as success never happens by accident but by purpose. As we have a dream of GSI coaching, Denice also had a dream. She listened to Les Brown's tapes and attended seminars and listened to Zig Ziglar. She knew she could do the things she dreamed of after leaving their sessions.

It takes determination to carry out our purpose. She encouraged us to write down ten reasons why we must do what we were at the event to do and to focus on them. She said, "Tough times never last but tough people do" and she ended by reminding us of the words of Winston Churchill, "Never give up!" Everyone gave Denice a warm round of applause for the positive advice she gave us. People who were tuned in across the Internet heard the same advice. Denice has a CD with Les Brown called "Finding Yourself," which I purchased of course.

As Les came back to the center of the stage, you could see and hear how proud he was of Denice. He told us, "When things go wrong, don't go with them." A setback is a setup for a comeback. Whenever we speak with people or our clients, speak with power, feeling, and conviction. If there's no test, there's no testimony. When life knocks you down, land on your back, because if you can look up, you can get up. Everyone will experience tragedies or problems as a part of life, but when these life events hit us, we must have a strong foundation to rely on in order to get up and get going again.

Tell yourself, "I expect to be successful because I decided to take the GSI course to become a master coach." You've got to be *hungry*, willing to invest in yourself, willing to see yourself as already there.

The people that will be successful provide more service than they are paid for. Coach your people through when things go wrong. Help them through the tough times.

Les told us a story when he wanted to be a radio DJ. After being turned down several times, he finally got the chance to be a coffee boy. He took the job and watched the DJs do their jobs. One day, a DJ was unable to work. Les got his big chance. He was "ready and hungry." Les was supposed to call in another DJ but ended up spinning the records himself. He was determined and hung in there when the times were tough. He watched and waited, and when the opportunity presented itself, he took it.

Les left us with these words. He is dedicated to GSI's coaches and master coaches. He encouraged us to keep high standards. If you want a thing bad enough to go out and work for it and take the heat for it, with the help of God we will get it. He asked God to bless us and America.

Once again, after listening to Les and Denice, I knew I was meant to be at the BLASST event. Only a fool could walk away from this event and not do things differently. There are no secrets that these masters of motivation were keeping hidden for themselves. We were given the tools and given the motivation, it was up to each of us to have the desire and act on it.

Remember to write down your goals and your dreams. Post them where you can see them every day. If it's going to take several months or years to complete, break the tasks down into small pieces. Then with faith,

Hours of Pure Gold

get started. If you don't know how, find someone who does and ask questions. You will be surprised how willing others are to help you. For those who doubt and belittle you, just accept it for what it is and move onward and upward. Don't let fear eat away your dreams. You are capable and entitled to them. And don't be afraid to encourage a child to make good use of their time and talents. Children like to be encouraged even if you think they don't.

9

Do the Right Thing with David Lawrence

Gary met David Lawrence just a few weeks before the BLASST event. He was a guest on his syndicated talk show *Online Tonight* where listeners were able to hear Gary speak about the event and Gary Shawkey International Group of Companies. Gary told us that a person like David Lawrence could make or break a person instantaneously. David Lawrence is a man of ethics especially on the Internet. He's also the cool-looking guy you might see on an ad or billboard some day wearing tinted bright green sun shades.

David wasn't sure that he could tell us anything we hadn't already heard. He recited a poem and asked anyone who knew it to join in. It was a poem written by Robert Frost during a time when he was despondent, disgusted, and annoyed. If you are familiar with Robert Frost, the first line starts with "Some say the world is . . ." David asked how many of us are despondent, disgusted, and annoyed with what the Internet has become. How many times have we been subject to receiving spam and porn email or been hit by a virus? How many times have we responded to a website and been trapped by pop-ups over and over and not able to get out without restarting the computer? He advised us to hit Alt+F4 the next time it happens.

Mr. Lawrence wanted to leave us with one single tool that would serve us in everything we do as we market on and off the Internet. That tool is to put ourselves in the seat of our audience. Everybody we meet or have contact with is our audience. When marketing on the Internet, we can decide to be honest or dishonest, and he implored us to always be honest.

David Lawrence said if Gary Shawkey International would let him, he would ensure that we do not become a dishonest company. If we allow him to look at all the elements of our operations like the programs, marketing techniques, emails, and so on, he would not let us become dishonest.

David has firsthand experience with people whose identity and money has been stolen on the Internet. He gets constant calls from parents who are despondent from what their children find on the Internet. David has two young daughters, and he is very protective of them on the Internet. He doesn't allow them to use the Internet without adult supervision. He said letting them alone on the Internet is like handing them the keys to a car and telling them to figure out how to drive it.

David warned us about the clever hackers on the Internet who steal people's passwords then change them so the original user can no longer access their websites. The hackers would use other people's accounts to send out spam, hack further, and create additional problems. He wants Gary to ensure that the GSI websites are secure.

Each day, hackers figure out new ways to attack a system. I always think that hackers are such brilliant people, and if only they channeled their energies to good and positive things, the Internet would be one million times better than it is.

When we put ourselves in the seat of our audience, we have to question ourselves about what we do on the Internet. Should we pirate music because we're mad at the record company or because the CD is too expensive? Should we pirate movies because it was cool that someone sneaked a camcorder into the movies on opening night and recorded the movie? Should we then send these all over the Internet to our friends? If we put ourselves in the seat of our audience that we've just stolen from, would we like this to happen to us? It's immoral to take something that does not belong to you.

When we market on the Internet, we must make simple everyday choices, choices when we pick up the phone to tell someone about an opportunity. Do we exaggerate because of excitement or lie because telling the truth is not impressive enough and the sale won't be made? David really appreciated Gary standing on the stage and saying in front of everyone at the event and over the Internet that some things just didn't work out. Some people would not admit when an idea or program failed.

David advised us to let people go when they are not interested or do not want to be part of the team anymore. People will remember you for your honesty. Do the right thing. Put yourself in their position if you wanted to quit a program and wanted a refund.

David does not claim to be spiritual, but he believes the old adage, "Do unto others as you would have them do unto you." If we apply this to Internet marketing, we will be successful.

HOURS OF PURE GOLD

He recited another part of the poem, "It is going to end because people can do things, because they could and not because they should." This is what is destroying the Internet. His admonition to us is, "Do our jobs the best we possibly can, market our products because we believe in them, learn everything we can, fix the things that are broken, be ready to give a refund, and make sure our email lists are double opt-in subscribers. Double opt-in may create less quantity but high quality, and you lessen the risk of having someone there who doesn't want to be on the list.

In ending, David hopes that we question ourselves by saying, "What can I do to make sure that what I do to someone else I wouldn't mind having done to myself?"

Wow! That was real food for thought. We can take David's message and use it every day in our business and professional lives in everything we do. Let's all try to be ethical.

10

Change Your Economic Future with Jim Rohn

It's Saturday morning, February 8, a beautiful morning in Santa Clara. Having had such a splendid day on Friday, I was really looking forward to getting more information to motivate and encourage me in my Internet marketing endeavors. I was offered a ride to the convention center and attended the breakfast, where Jim Rohn and Bob Burg were the honored guests. I mentioned that I was currently reading some of Bob's books, so when he came and sat next to me at the table, I was grinning from ear to ear. I was so excited and happy to meet the co-author of *Gossip, Ten Pathways to Eliminate It from Your Life*, *Endless Referrals*, and *Winning without Intimidation*. It felt like we were old friends, and we talked and joked just as if we were. I told him I wanted to hear more about "sphere of influence" that I was reading about in *Endless Referrals*. I was able to get a photo with Bob, and that will always be treasured.

Hours of Pure Gold

I've heard on many occasions how well-respected Jim Rohn is by Gary Shawkey. I enjoyed listening to him speak to various people in the breakfast room. Having the best weekend of my life, I was really looking forward to hearing Mr. Rohn and understanding this special relationship Gary has with him.

After breakfast, we all went to the meeting hall and continued with the sessions. We had the pleasure of some fine advice from Gary.

Gary told us that success could only be by intention. What matters is how we feel in the "here and now." He assured us that whatever we put our mind on, day by day, we will achieve it. Gary encouraged us to have a journal, to make notes, to write down our goals. Keep the goals in front of you, review them regularly, and check them off when completed. Some goals may take years to complete. Gary mentioned that when he first started out in marketing, he went to one of Jim Rohn's seminars, and one of the goals he made for himself was to have Jim Rohn speak at one of his seminars. Almost twenty-one years later, he can check the goal off. I felt very touched witnessing this occasion, and everyone was so proud of Gary and what he has accomplished in his marketing career.

> *Jim Rohn devoted his life to a study of the fundamentals of human behavior and personal motivation that affect professional performance. A millionaire, entrepreneur, and businessman, he is devoted to helping others achieve all they are capable of in life and business. He has been hailed as one of the most influential thinkers of our time. Jim has helped to motivate and train an entire generation*

> *of personal development trainers, as well as hundreds of executives from America's top corporations. He can awaken the unlimited power of achievement within you!*

After Gary proudly introduced Jim Rohn to the stage, he made himself comfortable at a table. To his side were an easel and a large white notepad with markers for writing. I knew I was in for some heavy teaching.

Jim started right off the bat by telling us, "We get paid for bringing value to the marketplace." Value could be a product, service, or opportunity. The value determines the reward. He then asked what the minimum wage is, perhaps $5 per hour, and what the top earner's wage is, perhaps $63 million per year. How can a person change their economic future? How does a minimum wage earner get from $5 to $6? The answer lies with your personal philosophy.

You can:
a. wait for the government to change the minimum wage;
b. wait for the company to pay you $6 per hour;
c. go on strike and demand $6 per hour. This is risky, and you can't get rich on $6 per hour;
d. change your philosophy of performance.

He asked us if it is possible in America to multiply the minimum wage of $5 by ten to make $50 per hour. Yes, it is. Is it then possible to multiply by ten again, then by ten again and again and again? Yet it is. To climb the ladder of success, you must learn to work harder on yourself than you do on your job. When you work hard on your job, you make a living; working hard on yourself, you can make a fortune.

Hours of Pure Gold

In my life, this doesn't just relate to money; it relates to anything that I put my heart and mind into. The more I read, the better reader I become, the more I work at difficult tasks, the easier they become.

Jim said, "Success is something you attract by becoming an attractive person, not by something you pursue." From testimonials and from personal experience, we have enough information to conclude that it's possible to design, build, and live an extraordinary life. Jim Rohn's view of the twenty-first century is that there's unprecedented opportunity for everyone and keen competition in the world.

To work harder on ourselves and seize the opportunity to bring value and to be attractive you need to:

1. Learn more than one skill; learn multiple skills.

Below are some skills that have propelled Jim's success, and we are encouraged to grasp them and cultivate them as well for our own success, whatever that may be.

   a. Find a product to sell, start part-time, and learn to take care of the customer.
   b. Learn how to find good people.
   c. Learn to organize. Get people to work together.
   d. Learn the skill of recognition and promotion.
   e. Learn to reward people for the small step.
   f. Be busy giving recognition to others. You don't need it for yourself.
   g. Communicate. Learn to affect people with your language.
   h. Human words can create a different type of light. Words are like a light for your pathway, use them wisely.

He reflected on our coaching desires with Gary Shawkey International and looked at our success in three ways. When training, we show someone how to do the job; when teaching, we teach life skills by showing someone how to make goals. When learning how to inspire, we help people to see themselves better than they are; we inspire them into the person they can become.

Jim spoke of transporting our children into the future. He said, "Don't be lazy in language, pray to be gifted in language." I think that is an absolutely wonderful phrase. Isn't it pleasing and satisfying knowing that we can pray for anything? Pray to be gifted in language, and let the words that you speak be an encouragement to someone.

Jim encouraged us to multiply, to be fruitful, and to be productive. In coaching, we help someone to market correctly on the Internet. We become fruitful by helping others who in turn help others. We become productive Internet marketers. We also must be productive enough to survive. When we get married, we learn how to provide for someone else—our spouse. We then have children, and we must produce even more—now for our spouse and our family. We then must figure out how to produce more than what we need for our lives and our family. We must produce much more in order to live this higher life.

2. Not only should we learn more than one skill; it would be very useful to learn more than one language.

Jim encouraged us to give it as a gift to our children, to encourage them to learn more than one language. This will bring value to their lives.

A person's personal philosophy is the greatest determining factor of how his life works out. Personal philosophy is like a guidance system. The guidance system helps you see the dangers in life. We want to minimize these. The guidance system also helps you see the opportunities in your life. We want to maximize these. Jim said, "It seems like God wanted to make a great adventure for the people he created," that's why the guidance system works the way it does.

He talked about extremities like love and hate, and evil and good. We should love what is good and hate what is evil. Here's how we develop a guidance system. Take for example a sailboat. The sailboat needs wind to blow in order to go somewhere. Jim said, don't curse the wind but set the sail to go the right way. We must use our minds to think and process ideas and information to be better than we were yesterday. As humans, God has given us the ability to do this.

There are two primary ways to learn information:

a. We learn from our own experience. Jim encourages keeping a journal as journals are for serious students. Don't trust your memory. Record both negative and positive experiences. Learn how to turn a negative into a positive.
b. We learn from other people's experiences, both negative and positive. Jim reminded us that the Bible gives us stories on both sides, people to admire and people to despise. The Bible is full of warnings and possibilities. We need to read books about good people like Gandhi and evil people like Hitler to know good from evil.

We should pay attention and learn from what we see and learn from what we hear, but we should be a selective listener. Stand guard at the door of your mind and decide for yourself what to listen to and what not to listen to. What powerful words—"stand guard." This is excellent advice that Denice also gave us. I really appreciated Jim referring to the Bible. It was such a confirmation that God took me to Santa Clara for a purpose.

    3.   Learn more than one skill, more than one language, and read all the books you need to read to make your fortune. Profits are better than wages: wages provide a living, profits make a fortune.

After listening to Jim and taking notes, he's now considered my financial advisor. He explained things in very simple but effective terms. I learned so much from this man who has a wealth of information to share. I'm just so glad to have been a recipient of his teaching.

I pray that this writing will inspire you to work harder on yourself, to take the necessary steps to reach your goals and desires. Encourage your children to read and to make good use of their resources. Our children are our future.

Each week I looked forward to reading Jim Rohn's FREE ezine. I literally devoured the thought provoking information.

11

How to Cultivate an Endless Referral of Customers with Bob Burg

> *Bob Burg teaches companies and individuals how to apply and perfect two skills dramatically important to personal and professional success. These are "business networking" and "positive persuasion skills." He has earned acclaim for delivering his programs in an entertaining style while providing information that is hard hitting, immediately applicable and most of all ... profitable!*

At the time of the BLASST conference, Gary Shawkey had 102,000 people in his opt-in list. Bob Burg asked the audience how exciting would it be if every one of us had 102,000 people in their organization one year from now? Well, it took Gary many years, so I was very interested in hearing how this could be done in one year.

So just how does one go about cultivating a network of endless referrals? Bob asked, "What happens when we talk to people about our business and products and they constantly say no?" It can get discouraging and even depressing. We can get to a state where people may sense our desperation because we want someone to accept what we have to offer. We can get the feeling that we need them instead of them needing us. We kind of lose our posture. Bob defines posture as caring but not caring that much; in other words, you care about your prospects, but you do not get emotionally attached. You are able to move on.

To cultivate a network of endless referrals you must develop a list of names. The list must have quality and quantity, so when one person says no, you say *next*. You let the attachment go and don't beg. Your responsibility is to expose your services; the acceptance of these services is the responsibility of the prospect.

Bob defines networking as "the cultivating of mutually beneficial give-and-take, win-win relationships." He promises that when done correctly, with general caring of the other person, you will turbo charge quickly the vast amount of people in your sphere of influence.

Bob stated that he has never had an original thought in his life. There are so many people who have information that we can tap into like Jim Rohn. We need to listen, learn, study, and apply the information that is available to us. Using proven systems permits ordinary people to achieve extraordinary things predictably. McDonald's has a proven system, and if followed, the proprietor will not fail, but if the proprietor wants to do things his own way, he or she will most likely fail.

Hours of Pure Gold

Most people have a sphere of influence of 250 people. These are relationships with people who know you, like and trust you, and who want to see you succeed. Now get this, every time you meet one new person, establish and cultivate a relationship, and they get to know, like and trust you, you've increased your potential sphere of influence by 250 people. Do this with enough people on a daily basis, and in very little time you build an incredible list of contacts—your sphere of influence.

Prospecting and networking has to be fun without getting stomachaches and without getting nervous. We must feel good about the process and the people we are prospecting to. Prospecting and networking can take place at meetings, heath clubs, and social gatherings and must be done correctly. It must be done in such a way that the person being prospected doesn't feel threatened, tricked, or pressured.

Bob said, "No one will hang up the phone on you when they are doing the talking. There's no pressure." Suppose you are at a charity event or barbecue, and you do not know anyone there. You will notice small groups of people, and in each group there is a group leader, the person whom the conversation evolves around. As you are walking around, you watch and notice. Now how do you meet this person; you can't just barge into the group and introduce yourself. There is a system. You wait until someone leaves the group, and you make pleasant eye contact with that person. Don't stalk them; just give a nice smile. If the person doesn't respond in kind, they are not interested. You say *next*, and there's no pressure.

If the person does respond, just introduce yourself. Even though you want to begin prospecting right away, don't do it. Just speak briefly and focus on what the other person does. Ask feel-good questions that by their very nature make people feel good about themselves and about you.

Bob has ten networking questions in his arsenal, but you only need to ask a few as follows:

1. How did you get started in your _____ business? People like to answer this type of question.

2. What do you enjoy most about what you do? It's a question that establishes a know-you, like-you, trust-you relationship. It's another positive question that elicits a positive response.

3. This is a key question. How can I know if someone I'm talking to is a good prospect for you? By asking this question, we again show this person we are different. We are being *you* oriented instead of *I* oriented, and we are giving the person the opportunity to promote himself.

At this point, you should end the conversation and ask the person for his/her business card. Only give your card if they ask for it; it will probably get thrown away. Bob has a four-step follow-up system that he uses to follow up with your new networking prospect. Time was short, and Bob was unable to explain it to us. The good news is I have Bob's book *Endless Referrals*, and you can get a copy too.

When you move to the next person, they may have nothing to do with sales, but that's okay. You use the same system, just geared a bit differently. Ask about their family, occupation, what they do for recreation, and what matters to them. Bob calls this FORM.

I don't think Bob said this would be easy, but I would imagine it could be fun and get easier with practice. It's all in the doing, folks. You must make a change and do things differently to achieve different results. I think building solid relationships is important, and I am sharing *Hours of Pure Gold* with my sphere of influence in order to get the word out and to accomplish the task of helping others to help others.

Bob Burg advises all network marketers to listen to audios and videos as they help you to learn and take nothing away from you. Read books consistently. When prospecting, learn how to remember names—it's very important.

Before leaving the affair, go back and reintroduce yourself to the new people you met and introduce the new people to each other. Once the new people are speaking to each other, politely excuse yourself from their presence, and they will talk about you.

Bob spent a few minutes speaking to us on the topic of *winning without intimidation* and, yes, he has written a book by that very name. *Winning without Intimidation* teaches you how to master the art of positive persuasion in today's real world in order to get what you want, when you want it, and from whom you want it, including the difficult people you encounter every day.

Bob recognizes that Gary Shawkey International is a unique company with a great group of leaders creating more leaders. He wished all of us much success in our endeavors.

Now I know many of you reading this book have a sphere of influence. Just look at the emails that get forwarded and forwarded and forwarded displaying all the email addresses of the recipients. Sometimes there are several pages of these and one small message. Can I ask you friends and acquaintances to be careful, and when necessary use the Bcc option in your email program? The BCC (Blind Carbon Copy) option allows you to send emails to several people without displaying all of their email addresses. I would be eternally grateful if you would speak to your sphere of influence about *Hours of Pure Gold* and invite them to purchase their own copy.

12

Taking Risks with David Miln Smith

In stirring, inspiring presentations perfect for every type of business audience. David Smith weaves his remarkable, true stories of overcoming obstacles, taking action, and learning into embracing the unknown with passion, courage, and confidence. As one CEO observed, "To hear David Smith speak is to fall in love with life all over again."

Most of us will do almost anything to avoid admitting we feel fear. We procrastinate, delegate, delay, fan the flames of conflict, or regret inaction. According to risk-taking expert David Smith, fear can be a potent, life-giving energy that gets us to our goals if we understand what to do with it.

Hours of Pure Gold

Gary was very excited when he introduced David Miln Smith to the audience. He said, "This will be fun." We will learn how to take risks. David Miln Smith is an athlete, adventurer, and speaker who travels the world doing things that others want to do.

We watched a short video presentation of many adventurous expeditions of David. David said the classic idea of adventure is to do something unbeknown to you, like firewalking. Some of his own adventures include swimming under the Golden Gate Bridge, running a marathon through a desert, and swimming the Straight of Gibraltar.

David tests himself by doing so-called impossible things. This stimulates him, and he accomplishes his feats by focusing on what is needed to be done instead of having a fear of dying while trying. As an adventurer, he looks deep down inside of himself; he gets out of his comfort zone and tries new things. David said once you try something new and get a bit comfortable doing it you want to do a bit more, to take the next step.

In order to accomplish the impossible, we must have a purity of purpose, confidence, and intention. David spoke about our minds and how fast they are, much faster than we think. We must use our minds when faced with adversity or uncertainty and not let fear overcome us. He told us about an encounter he had with a crocodile when swimming on a beach in Costa Rica. When swimming back to the beach about two hundred meters from the shore, he looked up and a twelve-foot crocodile was staring him in the face with its jaws open. He was heading straight for the crocodile who was probably thinking David was his next meal. David had to think fast. He only had a split second to react. Four things were going through David's mind in that second:

First – Oh . . . !
Second – He could handle this.
Third – David suddenly felt bigger than he really was.
Fourth – He had to neutralize the crocodile's teeth.

He punched the crocodile right in the mouth; he had to hit him first. The crocodile bit his arm; he pulled it out of the crocodile's mouth then sprinted to the beach. David said the experience wasn't only about how fast our minds work but about perception. I think he felt lucky to be alive. What would you have done in that situation?

He told us about another experience when canoeing down the river Nile and being captured by Nubian crocodile hunters and hostile Egyptian fisherman who considered him an intruder. David certainly doesn't resemble an Egyptian. In this moment when fear could have overcome him, he again had to use his mind; he had to win them over. He had to communicate with them. He had to survive. He did this by mentioning the name of a famous swimmer and showing them a medal he won at a previous event.

Sometimes you don't have to face challenges or fear alone. The coaches and members of GSI are a team; we have support, and we can all help each other. Isn't that what life and unity is all about—helping and supporting each other. David encouraged us to do the things we want to do and to be *outstanding* when doing them as tomorrow is not promised to anyone.

Being an entrepreneur requires energy and enthusiasm and taking risks. For some people, taking risks sets off mental alarms and prevents them from reaching their goals. If you look at bankers, they derive profits from taking risks. Risks have unknown outcomes. People don't take risks because of *fear*; fear of failure, fear of success, fear of loss, fear of embarrassment. It is our perception that triggers fear. If you want something to change in your life or your job, you must learn to release your fears; you must take the first step to do something about it.

As you read and accept the information from the various speakers, it's still only information and not skill. Skill is in the doing, like riding a bike. One usually learns to ride a bike in stages. What stage are you at in your desires and what stage will you be at three months, six months, and one year from now? The perception we have of things drives our behavior. We all grow up with certain beliefs. We play out these beliefs so many times in our heads, and we think they are real. We only see things through our beliefs. As we get more information on marketing and becoming successful, we begin to see things clearer and clearer. We may even say after a while, "Oh, that's how it works." You get an epiphany or a flash. Coaching others is a daily adventure, taking the information, becoming skilled at using it, and assisting others with their own adventures.

David asked the audience to shout out things that fear creates. Some of the answers were sweating, rapid heartbeat, fast breathing, a blank mind, rapid talk, nervous voice, doubt, and paralysis. Sometimes in coaching or anything we do to help other people, we experience *fear* of some sort. Once we've completed the task or practiced it a few times the fear lessens and eventually goes away. We must not let fear prevent us from achieving our dreams.

David told us of another encounter he had in Kenya with a lion. He told the definition of fear is:

False
Evidence
Appearing
Real.

There's a certain way to hunt a lion with a chant and a certain tool which he showed us. He also demonstrated to us the chant and the jump that the Kenyans do. Of course we all stood and started jumping and chanting the hunting sound. We all looked and sounded silly, I'm sure, but we had fun all the same.

David wasn't always successful. When he was younger, his lifestyle had something missing which prevented him from doing what he dreamed of doing. It wasn't until he made a decision to change, to take risks to focus that his life changed. When he said he wanted to swim the Golden Gate Bridge, people laughed at him and made bets that he couldn't do it.

He had to prepare by starting to swim one mile or fifty-three laps in the pool, swim in the bay to get acclimated to the water temperature. He could have been turned off by the magnitude of the adventure but instead worked on small parts at a time in order to get the full job done.

Since swimming the Golden Gate Bridge, he swam longer passages and even between continents Africa to Europe. He said the swells were like huge hotels, and the swim had been attempted nineteen times by others prior to him. I lift my head to David Miln Smith, and I was very proud to be in his presence. His experiences were great motivators for success in Internet marketing and any task I might take on in the future.

When I see young men and women wasting their lives by sitting on walls or fighting each other for no apparent reason, it hurts me terribly. If only they knew the potential they really have. We can't give up on our youth; they are the future of our world. There are too many overcrowded prisons. Let's be good mentors, and let's do our part to build healthy communities with rewarding services and programs. There are times when we just want to hang our heads and give up or say it's their problem, but God commands us to love one another, and we must put our faith and trust in him and believe that he will give us the wisdom and strength to forge on.

David said there will always be nay sayers, people who say things are impossible. You don't have to buy into what people say. Sometimes we have to go through systems and models, some are proven and some are not. To get the rewards, you must punch through. Joy is when you punch through fear. How great it is on the other side.

David Miln Smith is the author of three books. I purchased one called *Hug the Monster*, which focuses on how to live, how to embrace your fear, and how to live your dreams. *The Joy of Risk*, the *Thrill of Reward*. I encourage you to get a copy, you will not be disappointed.

My friend, don't let fear hold you back and prevent you from living your dreams. When burdens knock at your door and trials and tribulations come, ask God to sustain you and give you strength. God is King of Kings and Lord of Lords, the all powerful, all mighty one. As a true father to his child, he does love you and will always be there to guide and to provide.

13

Fundamentals of Success with Jim Rohn

We were introduced to Jim Rohn once again for his second session with us. I was more than ready to take in all his advice. My mind was like a sponge just ready to sup up the information. I could take this information and put it into practice or shelve it in the back of my mind. It's certainly not shelved as I'm sharing it with you.

Jim told us there are several books that we could read to help us in our marketing and indeed our lives, but if we don't read them, they won't help us. Sounds simple enough, doesn't it? Three books he recommends are:

1. The Bible
2. *Think and Grow Rich* by Napoleon Hill
3. *The Richest Man in Babylon* by George S. Clason

Hours of Pure Gold

You cannot begin to imagine how great it was to hear him say the Bible first. It is the first on my list as well. I have all three books in my library, so I guess Jim and I have something in common. I decided to reread *Think and Grow Rich* again, and this time I finished it. My desire for reading since the event surprises even me.

The Bible is the most wonderful book, full of real-life stories, stories of love, examples of how we should and should not live. The best story is about God who became man in the flesh, Jesus Christ, and dwelt among us. Just knowing that God loved you and me so much that his son had to die so our sins could be forgiven is the greatest testimony of love. As Dr. Dyer said, when we connect with God, have a relationship with him, there's nothing we cannot accomplish. God, the all-powerful almighty one can transform us from the person we are now to the person we are meant to be. It is this love of God that we need to share with our fellow men. The promises God makes in the Bible are worth more that any amount of money you can imagine or your wildest dreams.

Jim said, *financial independence* is the ability to live from the income of your personal resources. He stressed how important it is to put something away each and every payday. Capital is any value you set aside to be invested in an enterprise that brings value. We must learn how to make a profit.

If kids don't understand the difference between easy and hard, they will think what is hard is easy. The difference between the rich and poor is that the poor don't look for the book. What's easy to do is easy not to do. Isn't that the truth? How many times do we put off doing the easiest of tasks or chores or reading a book we've purchased?

Personal development is the secret to wealth, happiness, and fame. Jim continued to speak to us about the fundamentals of success.

1. Personal philosophy. I wrote about this in chapter 10, "Change Your Economic Future."
2. Attitude.
   How you feel:
   a. about the past - borrow lessons from the past and invest in the future, for example, don't continue to make the same mistakes over and over;
   b. about the future (inspired by goals). In designing the next ten years of your life, decide what you want, whom you want to meet, where you want to go, what your health goals are and your goals for your children. Write them down, and when they are met, check them off the list, then celebrate. Put everything on your list whether they are small or big;
   c. about yourself, your self-esteem.

What type of power would you like to achieve? How would you like to help someone? How do you feel about everybody? Each of us needs all of us, and all of us need each of us. In our communities, are we going to complain when things are not going as we would like them to, or are we going to try and be a positive influence to those around us and look for ways to be a part of the solution?

Jim said we need to learn to appreciate everybody's gifts. One person doesn't make an economy. One person doesn't make an enterprise. It takes people behind the scenes as well.

3. Activity – what you do and the actions you take. He said the doing finishes the miracle and gave us the example of a mother in labor. I can speak from experience after having two natural births myself. After all the back pain, the crying, the clenching of anything within reach, the pushing, a beautiful new life is brought into the world, the miracle of birth. So yes, coaching and marketing will take work and possibly hard work, times when you want to give up and cry, but for those who stay the course, the results will come.

Jim told us to affirm when we are broke, and the truth will set us free. I wrote in my book, "I live in Bermuda and I'm forty and I'm broke." Well I'm not really broke; I'm extremely blessed, and I have lots to be thankful for. Affirming the truth helps us to correct the errors in judgment and helps us to set up new career disciplines. Let's play out an error in judgment scene. The names used are fictitious.

Mary is speaking to John about her wage.

Mary: The wage I make is all that the company pays!
John: No, Mary. That's all the company pays . . . *you*!

Are you getting your worth in pay? What value are you bringing to the job? This made me think seriously about the actions I need to take to become a valuable coach, of being an Internet marketer and about my current job as well.

Mary: That's too expensive!
John: No, Mary, you just can't afford it.

The next note in my book was, "Write a book—My Weekend with the Masters." Jim reminded us that if we change, everything will change for us. There are six days to work and one day to rest, and he told us not to get those numbers mixed up. Six to one is better; if you rest too long, the weeds take over the garden. Six out of seven days of our teaching and training should be about labor. There are multiple advantages to having the seventh day for religion, rest, family, evaluating, and looking forward to the next six days.

Jim gave us lots of examples of how change can make the difference between success and failure. A goose can't go north because it is a goose. We as humans can decide which way we want to go. Jim Rohn spent the first six years in business broke, the second six years he wound up rich because he discovered he was not a goose. He made a change and did something different from the first six years. I vowed to make some changes in my Internet marketing to have better success.

Jim said, "A miracle is simply something we don't understand how it happens." Wisdom and faith must include work. Work is required to build a cathedral; work is required to build a country. When we work, instead of saying thank God it's Friday, say thank God it's Monday. Now that's a change of attitude.

You must measure progress. To make reasonable progress in reasonable time, you must be reasonable with time. Reasonable times are at the end of the day. Measure by not carrying anger over the next day or week. You get paid at the end of the week after the work is done.

Success is a numbers game; don't make the same mistakes you made ten years ago. Again, Jim used some examples.

Mary:	John, how many books have you read in the last 190 days?
John:	None, Mary.
Mary:	Not a good number, John. How many classes have you attended?
John:	None.
Mary:	In the last six years you've been working, how much money have you saved?
John:	Not much.
Mary:	If these numbers don't change, John, you won't change.

Each of us in our personal lives need to pick some easy numbers and make a change.

5. Lifestyle – this is the essence of it all, designing and living a good life. Some attributes of a good life are:

   a. Productivity – designed for the 6:1 ratio of working six days. Jim said, "The sleep of a laboring man is sweet, not of a goof."
   b. Good friends – these are your best support system.
   c. Your culture, your heritage, and keeping it alive.
   d. Your spirituality – belief in God. Jim asked, "How come America does so well? Just read the money." When we can't pray in schools, just tack up the money. We must study, practice, and teach what we believe to our children, our spouse, and our friends. We need to turn off the television and go out and do something meaningful.

Jim told us about a story that he told his wife. He said, "When I make some money and lots of it, when we go to the restaurant, we order our meals from the left side. Don't look to the right." I had to think about this for a minute, but when I caught on, it was a fabulous thought. We had a good chuckle over it when we met for dinner. Jim told us that God said, "If you plant the seed, I will make the tree." Are you planting the seed in your life?

It's certainly rewarding to me to know that when I work in earnest, in honesty and truth, and when I put God first, my cup overflows with joy, peace, and abundance. I'm looking forward to looking at the left side of the menu. There's a menu for you too; what side will you be looking at?

14

The Key to Success with John Amatt

Before Gary introduced Mr. John Amatt he told us this, "Today is the first day of the rest of our lives." When you think of that phrase, it allows you to put the past behind you and make a fresh start. He was encouraging us to take advantage of all the tools and advice that we received over the weekend, to build our subscriber base, to improve our relationships, and to expand our businesses.

I've told you about several wonderful acts of kindness I experienced at the event. Well, they continued. Gary introduced us to a lady and her family who were in the audience. Her name is Mrs. Lee Paterson, and she is the founder of African American Movers and Shakers. Mrs. Paterson wants to make a difference in the lives of children, mentoring, teaching, supporting, and loving them. She approached several organizations for financial help to get her program started and was turned down. Gary promised to help and gave her a cheque for $2,000.00 to get started.

He also promised to send twenty-five children from her group to an all-expense-paid trip to the camp for one week. Mrs. Paterson spoke briefly about her dreams and aspirations for these children, and she humbly accepted the wonderful gift from Gary. As Denice and Churchill reminded us, "Never give up."

> *"The key to success is preparation." Through an awe-inspiring, multimedia presentation, John Amatt relives his death-defying climb to the top of Mount Everest—inspiring success, professional achievement, and peak performance!*

I was quite eager to listen to the story of John Amatt who led the first Canadian expedition to the top of Mount Everest, the highest mountain in the world. It was late in the evening on day three, and I was starting to get physically tired, but my enjoyment of the event and the speakers kept me awake, and I didn't want it to end. The information was priceless.

After Gary introduced John to the stage, he told us a little about himself. He lives in the Canadian Rockies in a city called Banff. Although in 1982 he led a group to the top of Mount Everest, he wasn't always a leader. As a child, he remembers being shy, insecure, and didn't take risks. He now makes a living speaking to thousands of people.

It took John and his team five years to prepare for the excursion. John said his story of climbing Mount Everest can be used as a metaphor as we are all adventurers that will take us to the top of our mountains. To me that meant becoming a master in Internet marketing as I put into practice the skills and techniques learned at the event. He said, "It's when we are forced to struggle that we discover who we are, the person that lies within." The hardest part of obtaining a goal is taking the first step, especially when our minds are in turmoil and fear when doing something new. When we move toward and confront our fear, it moves away from us. Each speaker echoed this in their own unique way, and it must be true because they are all successful in their endeavors.

The team of climbers and the Buddhists Sherpers had to work as a team. There were strengths and limitations. They had to build on the strengths and challenge the limitations to accomplish the goal. The team had to be built on trust. He said when we take risks we stay focused. Climbing Mount Everest is certainly a risky challenge.

As you climb higher there's a lack of oxygen and a loss of weight. Things take longer to get done. You must have the mental determination to keep going even though your physical resources are being diminished. The climb is extremely dangerous. When there's ice falling down the mountain, tragedy can and does occur. His team tried to minimize dangers by fixing ropes and ladders on and across the ice as well as moving when the ice was less likely to shift.

He spoke of having a secure place to come back to recover, like returning home after a hard day's work. This security and renewal gives you the courage and ability to go further. To fulfill the goal of reaching the top, you must be committed and work as a team.

The climbers hiked with eight tons of equipment to the first camp site. After two weeks, everything was going well, and they started to fall into a feeling of complacency. The environment changed day by day. They encountered storms, wind, and an avalanche with nowhere to hide. Three of the sherpers died, and a few days later, one of the climbers died. A second climber almost died from a falling block of ice and was going to quit, but after a few days he decided to keep going, to fulfill the goal they spent five years preparing for. John advised us not to give up when difficult times come. Difficult times are a fact of life.

He reiterated what Jim Rohn told us, that our commitment to our goals is directly involved in our values and beliefs that are instilled within each of us. Although their goal was to ensure one person made it to the peak, it was the effort of an entire team that made it happen. It's important to recognize the efforts of the whole team. When John and the team reached the summit, the strongest person continued to the peak, the top of the world where beautiful pictures were taken. He told us how the photographer had to manually set the exposure on the camera at different settings to ensure the perfect picture was taken. He used the metaphor F8 and be there.

John said, "We must F8 our minds and expose it correctly to the changing world we live in and be there to meet the challenges. We must make changes as the world changes because the way we did things last week, last year, last millennium are not necessarily working anymore. Like I said, what works today in marketing may be old hat tomorrow, so we must be willing to make adjustments.

We build trust in each other when the times are hard. We all operate in different arenas. Attitude is the key to success, not skill, not knowledge, not education—*attitude!*"

The adventure attitude offers nine keys to happiness, fulfillment, and success in life, no matter in what arena of challenge you are operating. John gave us meanings to each of the letters in the word *adventure*.

A	Adaptability
D	Desire and Determination
V	Vision and Values

Hours of Pure Gold

E   Experience
N   Natural curiosity (as children have)
T   Teamwork and Trust
U   Unlimited optimism
R   Risk – ability
E   Exceptional performance

Everybody has it in them to be adventurous.

John Amatt encouraged us to "keep on climbing," and I encourage you climb to the top of your mountain and conquer that goal on your list. And when the going gets tough, stop—reflect, replan, if necessary, and improve.

After listening to John Amatt, we took a break for book signing. Everyone gathered in the foyer area and purchased various materials from the speakers, had pictures taken, and had books and CDs signed. When we resumed an hour or so later, Gary graced us and was very upbeat about everything. He was overwhelmed and was thankful for everyone's support. He reminded us of our teamwork and that as we continue to grow how important it will be for us to support one another and be there to help others.

Gary said that Jim Rohn and Dr. Wayne Dyer are both multimillionaires who have wives, children, and grandchildren. So why are they here speaking with us—not for the money. They chose to speak at the event because they believe in what we are doing, they believe in the people we have, in the concepts we teach. He encouraged us to be thankful for them.

Gary introduced to the stage our wonderful director of coaching, Dr. Sylvia Williams.

Sylvia said, "Do you feel the possibilities and the power here." Everyone was feeling something special; I'm convinced. I know I felt the power, and I clapped and said, "Yes!"

Sylvia reckons we are like a snowball rolling from the top of the hill, gaining momentum, getting bigger and bigger as it rolls and bringing in more and more people.

There was a lady named Gina who had a surprise for us. Gina is a registered nurse, and her husband is a master coach for GSI. Gina is willing to donate all her holiday time as a nurse at the camp in Ohio. Now that is self-sacrifice, and it was just another example of giving and love for other people. I had the privilege to have dinner with Gina on the last night—what a lovely person. Thank you, Gina.

Sylvia told us about the power of thinking. We program our minds to create our reality. There are two creations; first we have a thought or an idea, then as we think about them we begin the process of manifesting the idea. Each of us has the power to create.

Sylvia has a seven-volume book collection handed down to her by her grandmother called *The Secret of the Ages* written in 1926 by Robert Collier. One of the volumes that she was quoting from reinforced the principles of the power of thought that the speakers taught us throughout the weekend. We all have the power of the mind, and the most important power that we have is the power of love. Sylvia closed the night by acknowledging her husband in the audience and expressing her love for him.

15

Event Finale... Can It Get Better Than This?

February 9, 2003, will forever hold special memories and treasures in my heart. It was the last day of the BLASST event. We had our final master-coaching session with Gary and Sylvia. Sylvia reminded us that learning is an ongoing lifelong endeavor. We had a question-and-answer period, where people not only asked questions about the coaching program but gave personal testimonies of what the program means to them. Sylvia thanked Doug Castleton, our unsung hero who created the cover for our master coaches manual. Doug does lots of the graphics for our websites and works tirelessly for the company.

Georgia expressed that we are all family and that we care for one another. Heather, my coach, expressed her gratitude for Gary and for the opportunity to help others. Ed mentioned that one of our coaches, Doug, a dialysis patient, wasn't feeling very well, and we said prayers for him led by one of our coaches, Dove. I'm thankful that I'm involved with a group of people who are truly loving and caring individuals. Sylvia reminded us that when we work with our clients, we must be honest, direct, and kind.

Gary paid tribute to so many people who work for the company and who work with him daily. He owes much of his success to Jim Rohn, his admirer, and I could see why. The giving that was evident throughout the weekend continued right to the end with flowers given to Debbie, his personal assistant, and certificates to all the coaches.

There was a young girl who attended the event with her grandparents. Anna-Jean is her name, and she was given the first position in the BizOpp4Kids coaching program. This program when launched will teach teenagers how to start up, run, and market their businesses on the Internet. I had the privilege to have lunch with Anna-Jean, her grandparents, and my client on the last day. I was deeply impressed with the outgoing personality and personal accomplishments that Anna-Jean has acquired. I know she will be good mentor and coach to any teenager she becomes associated with.

The drum roll for the convertible took place, and a man in a wheelchair named Dale won it. Everyone was so happy for him and clapped and cheered as he put himself in the car. Believe it or not, Sylvia predicted that Dale would win the car and told him this before the draw took place. Amazing!

Just before the end, Gary made an emotional tribute to his wife, Stephanie, for all that she is to him and his family. Stephanie doesn't like a lot of fuss and attention. She likes to work behind the scenes. Gary asked all the attendees to gather out in front of the building because he had a special treat for Stephanie. We all went outside, and there was a white stretch limousine adorned by red roses. We formed an aisle for Gary and Stephanie to walk through. The staff was throwing out buttons, hats, and T-shirts. People were hugging and crying. It was so beautiful. When Gary and Stephanie came out, everyone cheered. They left in the limousine and headed to the Redwood Forests, somewhere Stephanie wanted to visit. It was just like sending the bride and groom off on their honeymoon.

Once they left, the group gathered to take a photograph and say our last good-byes. Some people were heading home and some were staying overnight and leaving the next day. I was one of those staying. A group of us had dinner together and shared jokes and thoughts of the weekend. One good thing was we would all meet again in PalTalk, but only now PalTalk would take on a whole different meaning for me.

The next day, I left Santa Clara at 5:00 a.m. and arrived back in Bermuda around 10:00 p.m. When I stopped over in New York, I had to change terminals, and I was able to go outside and touch the falling snow, a wonderful brand-new experience, a perfect ending to a great weekend. I just couldn't wait to tell everyone about the best weekend of my life and all that I learned.

Thank you, Lord.

16

The Story Is Told . . . The Journey Continues

After the event in Santa Clara, California, it was time to take all the knowledge and put into practice. Our regular Friday-night coaching meetings continued. The coaches that I met in California were no longer just voices in cyberspace; everyone was genuine and dedicated to helping others.

The first hour, Sylvia reinforced our company's purpose and values often referring to the teachings of the remarkable speakers. She always motivated and encouraged us to take our coaching responsibilities to the next level. The second hour was practical business and coaching lessons.

We had a coaching website that was constantly undergoing changes for improvement. We launched a *free* thirty-day ecourse to teach people how to market on the Internet. I got my second client and was on my way. Dr. Sylvia Williams, Ginger Geracitano, and Jill Hyland teamed up and created the GSI Xtreme eZine. The eZine was sent out weekly by coaches and master coaches to their opt-in subscriber list. It contained up-to-date information on what was happening with the company along with articles to help anyone in marketing on and off the Internet.

When I started writing the book, I drafted a project plan and wanted to have the first draft of *Hours of Pure Gold* completed by Easter 2003. This was a demanding schedule, but I set this date because I knew that I had to pack up my entire household and move out of my home to begin renovations. Anything I was working on would take a backseat during the move. When Easter arrived, I was nowhere near finished, although I worked on it early mornings and late nights consistently. I was determined to continue working on the manuscript.

May through July, so much was happening with the company. New programs were being developed and talks of mergers were taking place; you can say we were on a roll. During this time, I found it difficult to attend the weekly PalTalk meetings and was playing catch up on a regular basis. On June 14, 2003, Gary Shawkey and a team of firewalkers were going to attempt to break Gary's own *Guinness* world record for firewalking with a two-hundred-foot firewalk. The event was set up at the Hernando County Fairgrounds in Brookville, Florida. A&E television was on-site interviewing the firewalkers and was ready to film every step of the two-hundred-foot firewalk. But it was not meant to be, not on June 14 anyway. Thirty minutes prior to walking, a torrential rainstorm came and washed out the event. Gary said the storm was contained within a quarter mile radius of the fairgrounds. It just wasn't meant to be. Everything happens for a reason.

The ProMoney Search Program was launched in June 2003, and later had its name changed to PowereSearch.

Most people who are regular users of the Internet use search engines to find information on a particular subject, product, author, or just about anything. PowereSearch is a pay-per-click search engine.

On July 4, Gary Shawkey International cosponsored the nation's capital fireworks display in Washington, DC. This event was broadcast over the Internet, and Gary and a group of GSI members were on hand to take the GSI message to the world.

At the end of July, my family moved to my mom's house, which is also a busy household with other relatives living there. Moving a family into another household is a total sacrifice by the host family and which I am very grateful. It also identifies some challenges. One challenge for me was the persistent noise that several people living together can generate. I'm generally a quiet person who detests with a passion any confusion. I feel out of control, and I just want the noise to stop. Sometimes there's nowhere to go, to escape and have a moment of solitude.

This is when I put on my meditating CD that I purchased at the BLASST event. It immediately calms my raging spirit; it is my escape. It's here when I can listen to God's voice speak to my heart, telling me to be still, to be calm, to be at peace. It's here when I can share my desires and concerns with God and ask for direction. It's here when I can lift my dear family up in prayer. It's here when I know I have a purpose and that God will see me through the struggles of life. To God I give all the praise and glory, and I thank him for bringing Dr. Dyer into my presence.

At the end of August, just before leaving Bermuda for vacation, I picked up my third and fourth clients. I literally only had time to introduce myself via email. I couldn't wait to get back and start coaching them how to market on the Internet. I received my professional set of Master

Hours of Pure Gold

Coaching DVDs that were edited from taped footage at the BLASST event. They are a priceless treasure. It seems like every time I go on vacation something exciting happens with GSI. I was so close to finishing the first draft of the book. It was a very exciting time for me, and I anticipated finishing it soon after my return. There were some other big things Gary had been working on for several months which I expected to come to fruition whilst on vacation.

I happened to access my email at the Internet café on the cruise because I simply couldn't wait to get back home to hear the good news. To my total shock and surprise, some of these things would not happen. As I've mentioned previously, the Internet is forever changing. Our coaching program was suspended, why? Although its principles are sound, it wasn't having the effectiveness that was desired, why? The mergers would not materialize either, why? There was a lot of discussion happening that I was not a part of.

I knew once I got home I would get more information why certain plans did not materialize, and everything would be explained. Well, the best plans are sometimes changed without notice. I was unable to return home on the scheduled date and had to spend three extra days in sunny Florida. Bermuda was hit head on by category 3–4 hurricane called Fabian which took the lives of four people, one a friend, and created total havoc to the island's airport, structures, streets, and foliage. It was the worst hurricane to hit Bermuda in my lifetime. So, needless to say, once I returned home we had no electricity for a few days and had to deal with the aftermath of Fabian.

When I did eventually manage to attend a PalTalk meeting, so much had already happened with GSI. I had so much to get caught up on. I didn't like some of the news and from reading various emails, the situation wasn't looking good. It would have been easy to wallow in despair, to give up on many dreams, but I just couldn't. An upward climb it would be, but with God's help I'd make it. I remembered a sermon Fr. John preached on church leadership. He told us, "The higher the wages, the greater the taxes." He told us to be prepared when doing God's work, of all the attacks and obstacles that will come our way. I am reminded that the God I serve doesn't give up when the going gets tough. Many times he holds me up and carries me along the way. I also remembered the BLASST event and all it meant to me and the words "Never give up." I had to rely on the teachings and forge on. I had to trust and have faith in God's plan for my life.

I can say that Gary is not a quitter either. Gary's attitude during this very challenging time was to go back to basics with what worked in the past and rebuild from there. In order to do this he restructured and downsized parts of the company. He was still dedicated to the success of his affiliates and members.

When the situation seemed really bleak, Gary announced something *big* happened with GSI. Gary, the promoter, had to keep his mouth shut on this one for a while, but when the floodgates opened, Gary believed the hard work, the trust, the beliefs of all the members over the years would begin paying off. The members were getting excited again.

Gary Shawkey International aligned itself with a $2.4 billion debt-free telecom company that forecast it would grow to $10 billion in sales in the next twenty-four months. The deregulation of public utilities in the United States created this opportunity.

GSI had all the programs, tools, coaches, expertise, and indeed leadership to market the services and business opportunity of this company. It was deemed a win-win situation for everyone involved.

Hours of Pure Gold

Unfortunately, this too didn't turn out as many people hoped it would. Members began to get disgruntled and discouraged. PalTalk meetings as I knew them eventually dissolved and many former dedicated members stopped supporting GSI.

I wrote to Gary a few times as I was making progress with the manuscript asking for advice with certain legal concerns I had. At first he was responsive and supportive, then he stopped responding to my emails. While this bothered me quite a bit, it didn't deter me from reaching my goal. I may never understand why. Remember I said God rescued me. He rescued me from the path I was heading in. Gary always told us not to invest anything we didn't mind losing or put another way, could not afford to lose. Had I been duped? Someone was making a lot of money and it wasn't me. I have no regrets because I did learn so much about Internet marketing and coaching. These are valuable skills to have and skills that I use today.

Yes, my desires, my path, and my focus have changed and I'm truly thrilled. My cup overflows with joy. There's so much work to be done in God's vineyard and that's where I'm being led now. I am thankful that God has directed me in writing this book and sharing it with you. I know it has many purposes.

I would like to once again take this opportunity to thank you for your purchase of *Hours of Pure Gold*. I pray that its message has inspired you in some way and that you take advantage of the principles of success. Success is an option in your life. Get started today to reach your goals and live your dreams, and along the way help someone to reach theirs. It would create a better world for all of us. God bless you!

In closing, a personal prayer:

> *Heavenly Father, thank you for guiding and helping me to write this book. May all who read it be inspired and encouraged to fulfill their dreams and goals. Fill their cups and let them overflow. Give strength to the weak, and let them know of your presence always. Draw close to those who are unsure of their true purpose, continue to guide them and direct their paths. Even if there's one word that sparks a change, all the praise and glory is yours.*
>
> *I thank you for your church. Thank you for founding it, for purchasing it with the precious blood of your son, Jesus Christ. Not a building but a courageous body of believers who through the years have given their all to worship you. Help us to persevere, to endure life's trials and tribulations, knowing that with faith in you we can overcome any situation.*
>
> *Dear God, help us to remain as faithful and obedient servants; thank you for your many blessings. Strengthen your church and help us to be stronger than ever as we put our trust in you. Help us to be courageous to tell others about you and to love and help others always. These things I ask in no other name but Jesus. Amen.*

HOURS OF PURE GOLD

*So this is my story – Hours of Pure Gold –
Thank you for reading it.*

May God's many blessings be upon
you and those you love.

—Kandi

Author Bio

Kandi Aleene White was born on February 15th, 1961 in the beautiful islands of Bermuda. She is happily married to Morris and they have two adult children, Amber and Tristan. She's worked all of her adult life in Information Technology in a local bank. Kandi took early retirement in August 2022. Kandi's always wanted to be an entrepreneur and this desire led her into Internet Marketing and Coaching. She is fond of writing notes about events and special occasions. She keeps several folders of interesting information, articles, quotes, pictures and so on. Never in her wildest dreams did she see herself as becoming an author, but as the old saying goes, 'never say never.'

In 2009, Kandi also authored the Hours of Pure Gold – Kids Journal with prayers, poems and words of encouragement, and is a co-author in the Best Selling Series, Wake Up… Live The Life You Love book – In Service.

Kandi believes that everyone has a God given purpose in life. She prays that the speakers motivational stories and the proven principles of success would inspire all readers of Hours of Pure Gold to reach their goals and never give up on their dreams.

www.ingramcontent.com/pod-product-compliance
Lightning Source LLC
LaVergne TN
LVHW020445070526
838199LV00063B/4851